Little House

Social Studies
Curriculum Guide

Spelling Bee participants: Jackson, Tori, Tanner, Rachel, Cameron

– Ron ©2005

written by
Mary E. Jeffries

illustrated by
Ron R. Jeffries

SCHOOL OF EDUCATION
CURRICULUM LABORATORY
UM-DEARBORN

Note for Librarians: A cataloguing record for this book is available from Library and Archives Canada at www. collectionscanada.ca/amicus/index-e.html

ISBN 1-4120-6013-3

For More Information

contact the author or illustrator at: littlehouse@nwglobal.com contact the editor/ technical coordinator at: info@nwglobal.com

Cover Photography

photographs are courtesy of

Ron R. Jeffries ©2005

Bridget Walker ©2005

Acknowledgements

cover design by Patti Vides ©2005

co-editors Patti Vides and Beverly J. Brown

technical coordinator Patti Vides

Copyright Information

Printed in Victoria, BC, Canada. Printed on paper with minimum 30% recycled fibre. Trafford's print shop runs on "green energy" from solar, wind and other environmentally-friendly power sources.

TRAFFORD
PUBLISHING™

Offices in Canada, USA, Ireland and UK

This book was published *on-demand* in cooperation with Trafford Publishing. On-demand publishing is a unique process and service of making a book available for retail sale to the public taking advantage of on-demand manufacturing and Internet marketing. On-demand publishing includes promotions, retail sales, manufacturing, order fulfilment, accounting and collecting royalties on behalf of the author.

Book sales for North America and international:

Trafford Publishing, 6E–2333 Government St.,

Victoria, BC V8T 4P4 CANADA

phone 250 383 6864 (toll-free 1 888 232 4444)

fax 250 383 6804; email to orders@trafford.com

Book sales in Europe:

Trafford Publishing (UK) Ltd., Enterprise House, Wistaston Road Business Centre,

Wistaston Road, Crewe, Cheshire CW2 7RP UNITED KINGDOM

phone 01270 251 396 (local rate 0845 230 9601)

facsimile 01270 254 983; orders.uk@trafford.com

Order online at:

trafford.com/05-0914

10 9 8 7 6 5 4 3 2 1

Table of Contents

Registration Information

Please take the time to register your copy of *Little House Social Studies Curriculum Guide* ©2005. By registering, you will receive free files of digital pages (in Adobe PDF format) so you will have the opportunity to print certain pages on your own printer. These files will be sent to you via email (PDF attachment, under 4 MB total file size).

Make a copy of this page, fill it out and mail (or email the requested information) to:

Mary E. Jeffries
307 S. Mt. Olive
Siloam Springs, AR 72761

littlehouse@nwglobal.com   (please use Subject: REGISTRATION)

Name:

Name of School:
(if applicable)

Grade Level:
(if applicable)

Mailing Address:

Email Address:

Personal information will not be used for any purpose other than to fulfill this order.

If you would like to be notified of updates to this book, please check here: ☐
If you would like to participate in teacher surveys (feedback), please check here: ☐

Your files will be sent to you via email within one week.

If you have any questions about my lesson plans or book, please feel free to email me any time.

Mary E. Jeffries

Little House Social Studies Curriculum Guide ©2005

About the Author

Mary E. Jeffries, M.Ed.

- received Master's degree in Elementary Education, Southwest Missouri State University, Springfield, Missouri, 2003
- received Bachelor of Science in Education degree in Elementary Education, John Brown University, Siloam Springs, Arkansas, 1975
- teaches first grade and has 24 years of elementary experience in private Christian and public education (12 years in each)
- was awarded Wal-Mart Teacher of the Year 2001
- received a national nomination for VFW Teacher of the Year 2001
- produced an "ARKANSAS CARES" video for PS234 elementary school, New York, in response to 9/11
- attends post-master's classes at SMSU, Springfield, Missouri
- resides in Arkansas with her husband Ron where they have lived in the same house for 30 years and raised five daughters
- has donated teaching services on numerous Indian reservations in New Mexico, Arizona and South Dakota

Personal Note from the Author

Having read the *Little House* (9 Books, Boxed Set) series to my first graders each year for more than ten years, I have developed my own state-standardized curriculum to go with it. With so many fun learning projects supporting the reading of the *Little House* series, I had a strong desire to share my insights with other teachers and students. The *Little House* books are timeless, classic reading for all ages and this curriculum guide will be an asset to learning in the classroom. My heart's desire is that you and your students benefit from these lessons as much as my students and I have.

Thank you to Dr. Dale Range, instructor at Southwest Missouri State University, for taking an interest in my work and believing it to be "phenomenal". Thank you, Dr. Range, for inspiring teachers to be a work in progress.

Thank you to my lovely grandchildren, Garrett and G. Rose, who were wonderful models for my book cover photographs.

This curriculum guide is dedicated to my mother, Rose (Rosella), who taught me that it is the everyday, simple things that bring joy to life.

Mary E. Jeffries

About the Illustrator

Ron R. Jeffries

Even as a teen, Ron was drawing and designing t-shirts in Long Beach, California, where he was born and raised. He has always had numerous artistic talents, such as drawing, painting, writing poetry, singing and playing a wide variety of instruments: guitar, tambourine, percussions, maracas, harmonica, rainsticks and congas.

He has been involved in many artistic projects including:
o designing and painting graphics at John Brown University
o participating in the *Chorale of the Ozarks*
o writing and playing music in coffeehouses
o playing percussion in bands

Personal Note from the Illustrator

I am illustrating this curriculum guide at the request of my wife who tells me that I am "the best artist she knows". She is a brilliant teacher and I believe in her work and in the values that it represents. The first graders of today will be our leaders tomorrow – teaching them about our history is the first step to preparing them for the future. Thank you, Mary, for giving hope to our next generations.

– Ron

Bibliography

Casey, B. (1976). *The Complete Book of Square Dancing*. New York, NY. Doubleday Publishers.

Collins, C. S. (2000). *Inside Laura's Little House: The Little House on the Prairie Treasury*. New York, NY. HarperCollins Publishers.

Collins, C. S. (1998). *My Little House Crafts Book*. New York, NY. HarperCollins Publishers.

Collins, C. S. (1996). *The World of Little House*. New York, NY. HarperCollins Publishers.

Faulkner, C.S. (music, 1850 / lyrics, 1947). *Arkansas Activity Booklet, The Arkansas Traveler*. Little Rock, AR. Sharon Priest, Secretary of State.

Gathrid, E. B. (1995). *My Little House Songbook and Tape*. New York, NY. HarperCollins Publishers.

Hackett, C. O. (1989). *Little House in the Classroom*. Grand Rapids, MI. Frank Schaffer Publications.

Mason, G. (1992). *Laura Ingalls Wilder Speaks (cassette tape)*. Mansfield, MO. Laura Ingalls Wilder Home Association.

Rice, D. H. (1998). *Across the Curriculum with Favorite Authors: Laura Ingalls Wilder*. Westminster, CA. Teacher Created Materials, Inc.

Stockard, J. W. (1995). *Activities for Elementary School Social Studies*. Prospect Heights, IL. Waveland Press, Inc.

Tunnel, M. O. (2000). *Mailing May*. New York, NY. HarperTrophy Publishers.

Walker, B. M. (1979). *The Little House Cookbook: Frontier Foods from Laura Ingalls Wilder's Classic Stories*. New York, NY. HarperCollins Publishers.

Wilder, L. I. (1994). *Little House (9 Books, Boxed Set)*. New York, NY. HarperTrophy Publishers.

How to Use this Guide

Materials Needed:

Reading the *Little House* (9 Books, Boxed Set) series pages listed for the week is the most important. The pages listed will be for one week, approximately 10-15 pages per day. The time it takes you to read those pages will fluctuate. Allowing just 30 minutes per day, the reading of the entire series can be accomplished in one school year. The activity can be done any day during the week. The days you do not use the activity given, you may accomplish Social Studies Standards in numerous ways: re-telling a story, journaling, drawing pictures to show comprehension creating sentences using first-next-last. Be creative, as the possibilities are endless! Listen to your students' input. There are student activity worksheets matching the lesson plan illustrations at the back of this curriculum guide.

Introduction:

You might use supplementary materials (sources listed) various times during the week to emphasize the learning.

Major Instructional Sequence:

Definitions and extra information are useful to the learning process. Modeling is a very important part of the process of teaching/learning (modeling definition: teacher shows students exactly what he/she means, demonstrates). Asking questions for understanding is not only assisting in learning but also accomplishing state standards.

Concluding Sequence:

The weekly activity may be varied according to what materials and supplies you have available. You should also consider what is age-appropriate.

Evaluation:

Student Scoring Guide: you may read the Scoring Guide to the students at the end of the learning process and give them time to decide whether they thought they did their best or not. Supply crayons or stickers for the happy/sad faces. Stress the fact that work does not have to be perfect!
Teacher Scoring Guide: you may use for keeping student records, portfolios, parent-teacher conferences, supplemental information for progress reports or report cards.

Other Notes:

A climactic event for the year is the *Little House* dinner (Lesson 32). For the dinner event, along with bringing the *Little House* foods, be sure to dress up for fun in *Little House* clothes:

o   Boys: overalls, suspenders, Dad's old flannel shirt, boots (or barefoot), belt buckle, straw hats
o   Girls: Mom's old dress over your clothes, bonnets, aprons, collars, handkerchiefs, Sunday shoes (or barefoot), braids

Whenever you read "Pa plays the fiddle," play a fiddle song from *My Little House Songbook and Tape*.

Most of all, remember to have fun and be creative!

Table of Contents (Lesson Plans)

Lesson Plan

Title:	**Lesson 1 - Identify Vegetables**

Date:		Grade:	K-4

Suggested Season / Date: Autumn / September, week 1

Time: 30 minutes (approx.)

Subject: Social Studies, Interdisciplinary Activities

Learning Style / Different Multiple Intelligences: Tactile/Kinesthetic; Naturalistic Intelligence (activity could be used for all areas)

Example: touching, tasting and seeing garden vegetables

Materials Needed:

1) *Little House in the Big Woods*, pages 1-59
2) *Little House in the Classroom*, page 20
3) *The World of Little House*, pages 13-20
4) *Inside the World of Little House*, pages 43-46
5) *Activities for Elementary School Social Studies*, pages 7.20-7.21
6) *Little House Social Studies Curriculum Guide*, Activity, Performance Assessment Task, Student Scoring Guide, Teacher Scoring Guide: Lesson 1 - Identify Vegetables

Introduction:

1) Read from *Little House in the Big Woods*.
2) Share information about Laura's garden from other sources.
3) The purpose is to introduce what Laura and her family grew in the garden.

Major Instructional Sequence:

4) Provide information about gardening. State definitions needed.

Little House Social Studies Curriculum Guide ©2005

5) Modeling: Provide examples available from garden as beets, cucumbers, squash, radishes, green peppers, tomatoes and okra. Talk about garden foods listed in story: pumpkins, squash, red and green peppers, potatoes, carrots, beets, turnips, cabbage and onions.

6) Ask question about garden vegetables for understanding.

Concluding Sequence/Closure:

7) *Little House Social Studies Curriculum Guide*, Activity: Lesson 1 - Identify Vegetables

Evaluation:

8) *Little House Social Studies Curriculum Guide*, Performance Assessment Task, Student Scoring Guide, Teacher Scoring Guide: Lesson 1 - Identify Vegetables

Alignment to State Standards:

(compare to standards shown: Arkansas)

Strand 3:	Production, Distribution and Consumption
Content Standard 1:	Students will demonstrate an understanding that different economic systems and limited resources influence cooperation and conflict in decision making.

Learning Expectations

PDC.1.2	Apply the concept that goods and services are limited by available resources, requiring individuals and societies to make choices.
PDC.1.8	Demonstrate an understanding of economic terms, such as production.
PDC.1.11	Determine how natural, human and capital resources are used to produce goods and services.

Rm ©2005

Activity

Title:
Lesson 1 - Identify Vegetables

Sources:

1) *Activities for Elementary School Social Studies*, pages 7.20-7.21 Adaptation

Materials Needed:

1) assortment of vegetables such as beets, cucumbers, squash, radishes, tomatoes, okra and potatoes
2) napkins
3) paper plates
4) serving tray for vegetables

Objectives:

As a result of this activity, the student will:
o recognize a vegetable as a cultivated plant, such as root of a beet
o identify various vegetables by taste

Introduction:

1) Show and identify each vegetable.
2) Show and identify vegetables cut up into small pieces on the tray.

Major Instructional Sequence:

3) Place pieces of each kind of vegetable on a serving tray.
4) Let each student experience touching, smelling and tasting a vegetable piece.

Concluding Sequence/Closure:

5) Lead in a discussion of how the various vegetables taste. Let them describe the taste of their favorite vegetable, their least favorite and the like.
6) Give opportunity for writing descriptive statements about one or more vegetables, such as how they look, taste and feel.
7) Give opportunities for artwork where students may draw vegetables, vegetable gardens and the like.

Little House Social Studies Curriculum Guide ©2005

Performance Assessment Task

Title:	**Lesson 1 - Identify Vegetables**

Name:		Grade:	K-4
Date:		Subject:	Social Studies

Alignment to State Standards:
(minimum of three standards, input State standards below)

Code	Standard Description

Description of Performance Task:
(include time, student performance, assessment)

Time:	30 minutes (approx.)
Activity:	Activity will correlate with reading *Little House in the Big Woods*.
Task:	o Student will view and identify vegetables directly from the garden: beets, potatoes, cucumbers, squash, zucchini, tomatoes or okra (vegetables available in season). o Student will use senses for activity: touch, smell and taste. o Student will have opportunity for writing, descriptive sentences and artwork.

Student Scoring Guide: (attach a copy)

Teacher Scoring Guide: (attach a copy of scoring key)

Score (select one): [4] Exemplary [3] Proficient [2] Apprentice [1] Novice

Student Scoring Guide

Title: | **Lesson 1 - Identify Vegetables**

Name:

☺☹ I identified each garden vegetable.

☺☹ I examined the vegetables through my senses.

☺☹ I recognized the vegetable as a cultivated plant.

☺☹ I differentiated between garden vegetables.

☺☹ I shared what I learned about garden vegetables.

Little House Social Studies Curriculum Guide ©2005

Teacher Scoring Guide

Title: | **Lesson 1 - Identify Vegetables**

[4] Exemplary	o Appropriately contrasts vegetables directly from the garden. o Effectively compares garden vegetables through use of senses. o Consistently concludes between vegetable pieces on a tray. o Creatively shares about garden vegetables.
[3] Proficient	o Reasonably deduces vegetables directly from the garden. o Clearly differentiates garden vegetables through use of senses. o Consistently demonstrates understanding of vegetable pieces on a tray. o Fluently shares about garden vegetables.
[2] Apprentice	o Not clear discussing vegetables directly from the garden. o Not much information explaining garden vegetables through use of senses. o Inconsistent generalizing about vegetable pieces on a tray. o Weak progression discriminating while sharing about garden vegetables.
[1] Novice	o Unclear identifying vegetables directly from the garden. o Very little describing garden vegetables through use of senses. o Little or no listing of vegetable pieces on a tray. o Serious errors naming garden vegetables.

Lesson Plan

Title:	**Lesson 2 - Ma's Clove Apple**

Date:		Grade:	K-4

Suggested Season / Date: | Autumn / September, week 2

Time: | 30 minutes (approx.)

Subject: | Social Studies, Sociology Activities

Learning Style / Different Multiple Intelligences: | Tactile/Kinesthetic; Visual/Spatial Intelligences (activity could be used for all areas)

Example: | touching, seeing, smelling cloves and apples

Materials Needed:

1) *Little House in the Big Woods*, pages 60-119
2) *The World of Little House*, page 21
3) *Activities for Elementary School Social Studies*, pages 4.12-4.13 Adaptation
4) *Little House Social Studies Curriculum Guide*, Activity, Performance Assessment Task, Student Scoring Guide, Teacher Scoring Guide: Lesson 2 - Ma's Clove Apple

Introduction:

1) Read from *Little House in the Big Woods*.
2) Share information about clove apple from other sources.
3) The purpose is to introduce a cultural Christmas gift, a clove apple.

Major Instructional Sequence:

4) Explain concept of clove apple.
5) Model and give example of clove apple.

6) Ask questions for understanding.

Concluding Sequence/Closure:

7) *Little House Social Studies Curriculum Guide*, Activity: Lesson 2 - Ma's Clove Apple

Evaluation:

8) *Little House Social Studies Curriculum Guide*, Performance Assessment Task, Student Scoring Guide, Teacher Scoring Guide: Lesson 2 - Ma's Clove Apple

Alignment to State Standards:

(compare to standards shown: Arkansas)

Strand 2:	People, Places and Environments
Content Standard 1:	Students will demonstrate an understanding that people, cultures and systems are connected and that commonalities and diversities exist among them.

Learning Expectations

PPE.1.1	Investigate how members of a family, school, community, state, nation and culture depend on each other.
PPE.1.2	Compare and contrast similarities and differences in cultures through a variety of experiences, such as reading, writing, drawing, role-playing, dance, music and simulation.
PPE.1.3	Analyze the contributions of various groups to community, state and nation.

Activity

Title: | **Lesson 2 - Ma's Clove Apple**

Sources:

1) *Activities for Elementary School Social Studies*, pages 4.12-4.13 Adaptation

Materials Needed:

1) ½ cup whole cloves per student
2) an apple or orange (one per student)
3) toothpick (optional)
4) cinnamon
5) plastic bags (large enough for an apple)
6) ribbon or wide yarn

Objectives:

As a result of this activity, the student will:
o make a clove apple
o create a design on the apple
o identify the smell and feel of the cloves on the apple

Introduction:

1) Discuss Laura's Christmas with extended family.
2) Share different ideas that might occur in the setting.
3) Tell students they will make their own clove apple.

Major Instructional Sequence:

4) Student will hold the round part of the clove and stick the stem in to the apple.
5) Student will continue to design the apple with cloves.
6) Student will wrap ribbon around the clove apple for hanging.
7) Student will put cinnamon in plastic bag.
8) Student will display in a plastic bag to later be used for smelling good in a closet.

Concluding Sequence/Closure:

9) Let each student show their clove apple and tell about their design.
10) Display the clove apples on a shelf.

Little House Social Studies Curriculum Guide ©2005

Performance Assessment Task

Title: **Lesson 2 - Ma's Clove Apple**

Name: _____ Grade: K-4

Date: _____ Subject: Social Studies

Alignment to State Standards:
(minimum of three standards, input State standards below)

Code	Standard Description

Description of Performance Task:
(include time, student performance, assessment)

Time: 30 minutes (approx.)

Activity: Activity will correlate with reading *Little House in the Big Woods*.

Task:
- o Student will identify and understand uses of clove apple.
- o Student will organize cloves on an apple.
- o Student will share about the design on the clove apple
- o Student will display clove apple

Student Scoring Guide: (attach a copy)

Teacher Scoring Guide: (attach a copy of scoring key)

Score (select one): [4] Exemplary [3] Proficient [2] Apprentice [1] Novice

Student Scoring Guide

Title: | **Lesson 2 - Ma's Clove Apple**

Name:

☺☹   I identified the smell and feel of cloves and apples.

☺☹   I demonstrated a clove apple by using cloves on an apple.

☺☹   I organized a pattern using cloves on an apple.

☺☹   I shared about my design of the clove apple.

☺☹   I displayed my clove apple.

Little House Social Studies Curriculum Guide ©2005

Teacher Scoring Guide

Title: | **Lesson 2 - Ma's Clove Apple**

[4] Exemplary	o Consistently concludes that cloves on an apple creates a clove apple.
	o Handles well designing a pattern of cloves on an apple.
	o Contains few errors summarizing a design of cloves on an apple.
	o Effective display of a clove apple.

[3] Proficient	o Clearly illustrates that cloves on an apple creates a clove apple.
	o Generally uses and demonstrates a pattern of cloves on an apple.
	o Appropriately shares a design of cloves on an apple.
	o Reasonable display of a clove apple.

[2] Apprentice	o Not much information explaining that cloves on an apple creates a clove apple.
	o Inconsistent creating a pattern of cloves on an apple.
	o Not too clear discussing a design of cloves on an apple.
	o Not elaborate display of a clove apple.

[1] Novice	o Lacks evidence describing that cloves on an apple creates a clove apple.
	o Very little understanding a pattern of cloves on an apple.
	o Unclear selecting a design of cloves on an apple.
	o Random display of a clove apple.

Lesson Plan

Title:	**Lesson 3 - Square Dancing**

Date:		Grade:	K-4

Suggested Season / Date:	Autumn / September, week 3

Time:	30 minutes (approx.)

Subject:	Social Studies, Interdisciplinary Activities

Learning Style / Different Multiple Intelligences:	Tactile/Kinesthetic; Musical/Rhythmic Intelligences (activity could be used for all areas)

Example:	hands on moving, dancing and touching/listening to music, sounds, rhythms and patterns

Materials Needed:

1) *Little House in the Big Woods*, pages 120-179
2) *Little House in the Classroom*, page 35
3) Song: "The Arkansas Traveler"
4) *The Complete Book of Square Dancing*
5) *Activities for Elementary School Social Studies*, pages 7.3-7.4
6) *Little House Social Studies Curriculum Guide*, Activity, Performance Assessment Task, Student Scoring Guide, Teacher Scoring Guide: Lesson 3 - Square Dancing

Introduction:

1) Read from *Little House in the Big Woods*.
2) Discuss square dancing, spaces, sounds and rhythms.
3) The purpose is to learn and participate in square dancing.

Major Instructional Sequence:

4) Provide information about Laura's extended family having a party and square dancing.
5) Modeling square dancing.
6) Ask questions for understanding.

Concluding Sequence/Closure:

7) *Little House Social Studies Curriculum Guide*, Activity: Lesson 3 - Square Dancing

Evaluation:

8) *Little House Social Studies Curriculum Guide*, Performance Assessment Task, Student Scoring Guide, Teacher Scoring Guide: Lesson 3 - Square Dancing

Alignment to State Standards:

(compare to standards shown: Arkansas)

Strand 2:	People, Places & Environments
Content Standard 1:	Students will demonstrate an understanding that people, cultures and systems are connected and that commonalities and diversities exist among them.

Learning Expectations

PPE.1.2	Compare and contrast similarities and differences in cultures through a variety of experiences, such as reading, writing, drawing, role-playing, dance, music and simulation.
PPE.1.4	Use student, family and community resources to recognize and understand the ethnic, racial and religious diversity of the United States.
PPE.1.5	Analyze the effects of interactions between people and their environment.

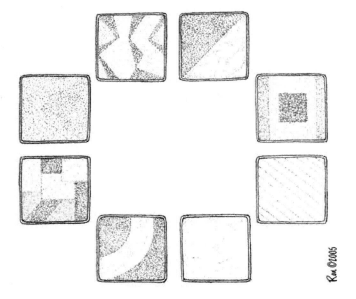

Activity

| Title: | **Lesson 3 - Square Dancing** |

Sources:

1) *Activities for Elementary School Social Studies*, pages 7.3-7.4 Adaptation

Materials Needed:

1) Carpet squares
2) Square dance partner
3) *The Complete Book of Square Dancing*

Objectives:

As a result of this activity, the student will:
o Determine spatial relationship to objects and other people.
o Describe self in spatial relationship to objects and other people.
o Use carpet squares to verify spatial relationships.

Introduction:

1) Determine carpet square spacing for partners and others for square dancing.
2) Each time will be stepping around the spacing.
3) Look at the spacing between squares and partner.
4) Have students identify the relationships between squares and partner.

Major Instructional Sequence:

5) Determine where squares should be placed to form square dance.
6) Make sure all students have opportunity to step in special areas.
7) Look at squares for spacing, forming the square for square dancing.
8) Have students identify spacing for partners for square dancing, each having their own space.

Concluding Sequence/Closure:

9) Place groups of eight students on carpet squares and let them practice square dancing to the music.
10) Let groups perform and share about square dancing.

Performance Assessment Task

Title:	**Lesson 3 - Square Dancing**		

Name:		Grade:	K-4
Date:		Subject:	Social Studies

Alignment to State Standards:
(minimum of three standards, input State standards below)

Code	Standard Description

Description of Performance Task:
(include time, student performance, assessment)

Time:	30 minutes (approx.)
Activity:	Activity will correlate with reading *Little House in the Big Woods*.
Task:	o Student will differentiate about spatial relationships. o Student will place carpet squares, forming a square. o Student will match up with a partner. o Student will demonstrate and perform square dancing. o Student will share what they learned about spacing through square dancing.

Student Scoring Guide: (attach a copy)

Teacher Scoring Guide: (attach a copy of scoring key)

Score (select one): [4] Exemplary [3] Proficient [2] Apprentice [1] Novice

Student Scoring Guide

Title: **Lesson 3 - Square Dancing**

Name:

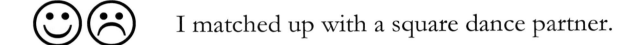 I matched up with a square dance partner.

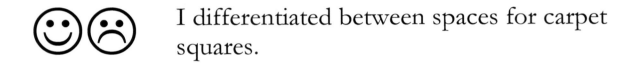 I differentiated between spaces for carpet squares.

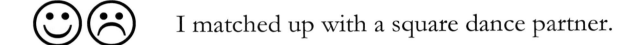 I used carpet squares to form squares.

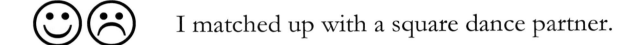 I demonstrated square dance steps.

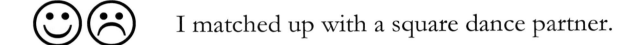 I performed square dance steps with a partner.

Teacher Scoring Guide

Title: | **Lesson 3 - Square Dancing**

| [4] Exemplary | o Appropriately decides on a square dance partner. |
| o Effectively compiles spatial relationships using carpet squares for forming a square. |
| o Consistently composes square dance steps with partner. |
| o Fluently performs square dance steps with partner. |

[4] Exemplary
- o Appropriately decides on a square dance partner.
- o Effectively compiles spatial relationships using carpet squares for forming a square.
- o Consistently composes square dance steps with partner.
- o Fluently performs square dance steps with partner.

[3] Proficient
- o Focuses on separating out a square dance partner.
- o Apparently deduces spatial relationships using carpet squares for forming a square.
- o Some errors demonstrating square dance steps with partner.
- o Reasonably performs square dance steps with partner.

[2] Apprentice
- o Not focusing on matching up with a square dance partner.
- o Significant weakness differentiating spatial relationships using carpet squares for forming a square.
- o Not clear on selecting square dance steps with partner.
- o Many errors with performing square dance steps with partner.

[1] Novice
- o Unclear about matching up with a square dance partner.
- o Serious errors outlining spatial relationships using carpet squares for forming a square.
- o Lacks recalling square dance steps with partner.
- o Very little performing square dance steps with partner.

Lesson Plan

Title:	**Lesson 4 - Braid with Straw**

Date:		Grade:	K-4

Suggested Season / Date:	Autumn / September, week 4

Time:	30 minutes (approx.)

Subject:	Social Studies, Anthropology Activities

Learning Style / Different Multiple Intelligences:	Tactile/Kinesthetic; Naturalistic Intelligence (activity could be used for all areas)

Example:	touching, doing and feeling, weaving straw from nature

Materials Needed:

1) *Little House in the Big Woods*, pages 180-238
2) *My Little House Crafts Book*, pages 12-15
3) *Across the Curriculum with Favorite Authors*, page 18
4) *Activities for Elementary School Social Studies*, page 3.26 Adaptation
5) *Little House Social Studies Curriculum Guide*, Activity, Performance Assessment Task, Student Scoring Guide, Teacher Scoring Guide: Lesson 4 - Braid with Straw

Introduction:

1) Read from *Little House in the Big Woods*.
2) Show different variety of straw mats and straw hats.
3) The purpose is learning to braid straw.

Major Instructional Sequence:

4) Show model of straw mat and hat. Explain concept of braiding with straw.
5) Model braiding the straw.
6) Check for understanding.

Concluding Sequence/Closure:

7) *Little House Social Studies Curriculum Guide*, Activity: Lesson 4 - Braid with Straw

Evaluation:

8) *Little House Social Studies Curriculum Guide*, Performance Assessment Task, Student Scoring Guide, Teacher Scoring Guide: Lesson 4 - Braid with Straw

Alignment to State Standards:

(compare to standards shown: Arkansas)

Strand 1:	Time, Continuity and Change
Content Standard 2:	Students will demonstrate an understanding of how ideas, events and conditions bring about change.
Learning Expectations	
TCC.2.1	Discuss and record changes in one's self, community, state and nation.
TCC.2.3	Use personal experiences, biographies, autobiographies or historical fiction to explain how individuals are affected by, can cope with and can create change.
TCC.2.5	Use a variety of processes, such as thinking, reading, writing, listening and speaking, to demonstrate continuity and change.

Activity

Title:	**Lesson 4 - Braid with Straw**

Sources:

1) *Activities for Elementary School Social Studies*, page 3.26 Adaptation

Materials Needed:

1) bundle of oat straws or a bundle of natural raffia (available in craft stores)
2) white thread
3) needle
4) scissors

Objectives:

As a result of this activity, the student will:
o produce a mat of straw
o develop an awareness of what Ma made from straw
o identify what can be made of straw

Introduction:

1) Show a model of a straw hat and straw mat.
2) Demonstrate how to braid with straw.
3) Tell students how to make their own mat of straw.

Major Instructional Sequence:

4) Assemble materials at work area.
5) Students braid with straw.
6) Students observe teacher/parents help with threading braid into a mat.

Concluding Sequence/Closure:

7) Let students show and demonstrate their mat of straw.
8) Place the straw mats in a classroom exhibit.

Performance Assessment Task

Title:	**Lesson 4 - Braid with Straw**

Name:		Grade:	K-4
Date:		Subject:	Social Studies

Alignment to State Standards:
(minimum of three standards, input State standards below)

Code	Standard Description

Description of Performance Task:
(include time, student performance, assessment)

Time:	30 minutes (approx.)
Activity:	Activity will correlate with reading *Little House in the Big Woods*.
Task:	o Student will describe and explain about braiding straw into a mat. o Student will braid with straw. o Student will observe teacher/parent sew straw into a mat. o Student will recognize straw forming into a mat. o Student will share about their straw braided into a mat. o Student will display their braided mat of straw.

Student Scoring Guide: | (attach a copy) |

Teacher Scoring Guide: | (attach a copy of scoring key) |

Score (select one): [4] Exemplary [3] Proficient [2] Apprentice [1] Novice

Student Scoring Guide

Title: | **Lesson 4 - Braid with Straw**

Name:

😊 ☹️ I described braiding straw into a mat.

😊 ☹️ I explained how to braid with straw.

😊 ☹️ I used straw for braiding.

😊 ☹️ I recognized a mat being formed by straw.

😊 ☹️ I displayed my straw mat.

Teacher Scoring Guide

Title:	**Lesson 4 - Braid with Straw**

[4] Exemplary
- o Clearly addresses designing a mat of straw.
- o Fluently formulates how straw is braided into a mat.
- o Uses and compiles straw for braiding into mat.
- o Handles well displaying mat of straw.

[3] Proficient
- o Focuses on developing a mat of straw.
- o Appropriately recognizes how straw is braided into a mat.
- o Fairly strong use of straw for braiding into mat.
- o Contains few errors in displaying mat of straw.

[2] Apprentice
- o Inconsistent explaining a mat of straw.
- o Not clear generalizing how straw is braided into a mat.
- o Significant weakness distinguishing straw for braiding into mat.
- o Contains some errors in displaying mat of straw.

[1] Novice
- o Unclear describing a mat of straw.
- o Arbitrarily defining how straw is braided into a mat.
- o Lacks selecting straw for braiding into mat.
- o Serious errors displaying mat of straw.

Lesson Plan

Title:	**Lesson 5 - Building a Log Cabin**

Date:		Grade:	K-4

Suggested Season / Date:	Autumn / October, week 1

Time:	30 minutes (approx.)

Subject:	Social Studies, Anthropology Activities

Learning Style / Different Multiple Intelligences:	Tactile/Kinesthetic; Visual/Spatial Intelligences (activity could be used for all areas)

Example:	touching and doing, creating and designing a log cabin from frosting and pretzels

Materials Needed:

1) *Little House on the Prairie*, pages 1-84
2) *Little House in the Classroom*, page 43
3) *The World of Little House*, pages 26-28
4) *Across the Curriculum with Favorite Authors*, pages 40, 47
5) *Activities for Elementary School Social Studies*, pages 3.20-3.21 Adaptation
6) *Little House Social Studies Curriculum Guide*, Activity, Performance Assessment Task, Student Scoring Guide, Teacher Scoring Guide: Lesson 5 - Building a Log Cabin

Introduction:

1) Read from *Little House on the Prairie*.
2) Show pictures, discuss and share information about her family living in a log cabin.
3) Discuss difference between Laura's home and students' homes.
4) The purpose is to learn about building a log cabin.

Major Instructional Sequence:

5) Show model of log cabin and examine it. Discuss differences between "then" and "now".

6) Model, allowing time for questions about building the log cabin.

7) Check for understanding.

Concluding Sequence/Closure:

8) *Little House Social Studies Curriculum Guide*, Activity: Lesson 5 - Building a Log Cabin

Evaluation:

9) *Little House Social Studies Curriculum Guide*, Performance Assessment Task, Student Scoring Guide, Teacher Scoring Guide: Lesson 5 - Building a Log Cabin

Alignment to State Standards:

(compare to standards shown: Arkansas)

Strand 2:	People, Places and Environments
Content Standard 2:	Students will demonstrate an understanding of the significance of physical and cultural characteristics of places and world regions.

Learning Expectations

PPE.2.1	Explain how geography and the environment affect the way people live.
PPE.2.2	Understand and apply the five themes of geography: location place, human-environment interaction and regions.
PPE.2.3	Compare and contrast the features of rural/urban.

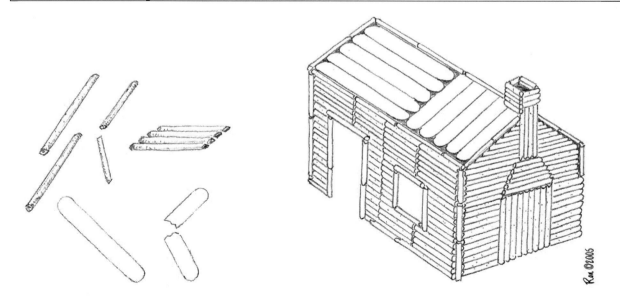

Title: **Lesson 5 - Building a Log Cabin**

Sources:

1) *Activities for Elementary School Social Studies*, pages 3.20-3.21 Adaptation

Materials Needed:

1) long pretzel sticks
2) frosting
3) small, clean school milk cartons (one for each student)

Objectives:

As a result of this activity, the student will:
o build a log cabin
o develop an awareness of different types of homes
o compare and contrast the differences
o identify the log cabin with a time and culture

Introduction:

1) Discuss Laura's Pa and Ma building their log cabin.
2) Show pictures of log cabins.
3) Show model of log cabin and examine it.

Major Instructional Sequence:

4) Each student will build their own log cabin using a small milk carton, frosting and long pretzel sticks.
5) Check for understanding and give assistance where needed.

Concluding Sequence/Closure:

6) Each student will display their own log cabin.
7) Each student will describe and share about their log cabin.

Performance Assessment Task

Title:	**Lesson 5 - Building a Log Cabin**

Name:		Grade:	K-4
Date:		Subject:	Social Studies

Alignment to State Standards:
(minimum of three standards, input State standards below)

Code	Standard Description

Description of Performance Task:
(include time, student performance, assessment)

Time:	30 minutes (approx.)
Activity:	Activity will correlate with reading *Little House on the Prairie*.
Task:	o Student will identify the log cabin with a time and culture. o Student will discuss Laura's Pa and Ma building a log cabin. o Student will use a small clean milk carton, frosting and long pretzel sticks to demonstrate a log cabin. o Student will share and display the log cabin.

Student Scoring Guide: (attach a copy)

Teacher Scoring Guide: (attach a copy of scoring key)

Score (select one): [4] Exemplary [3] Proficient [2] Apprentice [1] Novice

Student Scoring Guide

Title: **Lesson 5 - Building a Log Cabin**

Name:

😊😞   I identified the log cabin with a time and culture.

😊😞   I discussed Laura's Pa and Ma building a log cabin.

😊😞   I used a milk carton, pretzels and frosting to demonstrate a log cabin.

😊😞   I shared about my log cabin.

😊😞   I displayed my log cabin.

Little House Social Studies Curriculum Guide ©2005

Teacher Scoring Guide

Title: **Lesson 5 - Building a Log Cabin**

[4] Exemplary	o Effectively compares the log cabin with a time and culture.
	o Appropriately demonstrates use of supplies to build a log cabin.
	o Genuinely shares about building a log cabin.
	o Contains few errors in displaying a log cabin.

[3] Proficient	o Clearly outlines the log cabin with a time and culture.
	o Fairly strong illustrating use of supplies to build a log cabin.
	o Focuses on relating about building a log cabin.
	o Reasonable display of a log cabin.

[2] Apprentice	o Weak progression explaining the log cabin with a time and culture.
	o Significant weakness extending use of supplies to build a log cabin.
	o Not much information discussing building a log cabin.
	o Contains errors displaying a log cabin.

[1] Novice	o Difficulty identifying the log cabin with a time and culture.
	o Incomplete recollection for use of supplies to build a log cabin.
	o Lacks focus describing building a log cabin.
	o Very little identity displaying a log cabin.

Lesson Plan

Title:	**Lesson 6 - Replica of Animal Skin**

Date:		Grade:	K-4

Suggested Season / Date:	Autumn / October, week 2

Time:	30 minutes (approx.)

Subject:	Social Studies, Anthropology Activities

Learning Style / Different Multiple Intelligences:	Tactile/Kinesthetic; Visual/Spatial Intelligences (activity could be used for all areas)

Example:	hands on, doing and touching butcher paper to design, create an animal skin coat

Materials Needed:

1) *Little House on the Prairie*, pages 85-168
2) *Little House in the Classroom*, pages 49-54
3) *The World of Little House*, pages 25-28
4) *Across the Curriculum with Favorite Authors*, pages 9, 41
5) *Activities for Elementary School Social Studies*, pages 2.14-2.15
6) *Little House Social Studies Curriculum Guide*, Activity, Performance Assessment Task, Student Scoring Guide, Teacher Scoring Guide: Lesson 6 - Replica of Animal Skin

Introduction:

1) Read from *Little House on the Prairie*.
2) Discuss Osage Indians and their way of life on the prairie.
3) The purpose is to learn about Laura's family and their experience with the Osage way of dressing.

Major Instructional Sequence:

4) Provide information about Laura and her family living on the prairie. Explain about the Osage Indians living on Indian Territory.
5) Allow time for questions about the Indian way of life.
6) Ask questions for understanding.

Concluding Sequence/Closure:

7) *Little House Social Studies Curriculum Guide*, Activity: Lesson 6 - Replica of Animal Skin

Evaluation:

8) *Little House Social Studies Curriculum Guide*, Performance Assessment Task, Student Scoring Guide, Teacher Scoring Guide: Lesson 6 - Replica of Animal Skin

Alignment to State Standards:

(compare to standards shown: Arkansas)

Strand 3:	Production, Distribution and Consumption
Content Standard 1:	Students will demonstrate an understanding that different economic systems and limited resources influence cooperation and conflict in decision making.

Learning Expectations

PDC.1.2	Apply the concept that goods and services are limited by available resources, requiring individuals and societies to make choices.
PDC.1.3	Determine whether all people have the same needs and opportunities to meet those needs.
PDC.1.5	Identify economic interdependencies among community, state and nation.

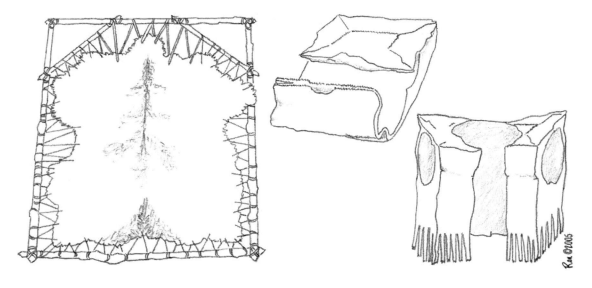

Activity

Title: | **Lesson 6 - Replica of Animal Skin** |

Sources:

1) *Activities for Elementary School Social Studies*, pages 2.14-2.15

Materials Needed:

1) butcher paper or large shopping bags (enough for each student)
2) scissors
3) paints
4) crayons
5) yarn

Objectives:

As a result of this activity, the student will:
o make a replica of an ancient animal-skin coat
o realize that some historical and present-day sources of clothing are plants and animals
o color and paint the coat to resemble the fur, skin and the like

Introduction:

1) Discuss this historical period and how people used clothing.
2) Explain furs were commonly used for clothing.
3) Explain Native Americans typically hunted buffalo, deer and elk for clothing and meat.
4) Tell students they will participate in an activity to make replica coats from animal skins like early human groups did.

Major Instructional Sequence:

5) Distribute materials and demonstrate how to draw the illustrated pattern on the butcher paper (or shopping bag) and cut appropriately to make a coat.
6) Students may paint and decorate by attaching yarn.

Concluding Sequence/Closure:

7) Have students don their coats and have a "show and tell" fashion show with each student modeling and telling about his/her coat.

Little House Social Studies Curriculum Guide ©2005

Performance Assessment Task

Title:	**Lesson 6 - Replica of Animal Skin**		

Name:		Grade:	K-4
Date:		Subject:	Social Studies

Alignment to State Standards:
(minimum of three standards, input State standards below)

Code	Standard Description

Description of Performance Task:
(include time, student performance, assessment)

Time:	30 minutes (approx.)
Activity:	Activity will correlate with reading *Little House on the Prairie*.
Task:	o Student will define the replica of an animal skin coat.
	o Student will discuss the historical period and how people used animal skin for clothing.
	o Student will use butcher paper to demonstrate a replica of an animal skin coat.
	o Student will paint, color and decorate.
	o Student will model their animal skin coat.
	o Student will share about the animal skin coat.
	o Student will display their animal skin coat.

Student Scoring Guide: | (attach a copy)

Teacher Scoring Guide: | (attach a copy of scoring key)

Score (select one): | [4] Exemplary [3] Proficient [2] Apprentice [1] Novice

Student Scoring Guide

Title: **Lesson 6 - Replica of Animal Skin**

Name:

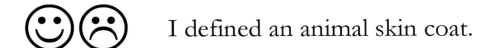 I defined an animal skin coat.

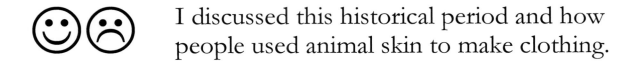 I discussed this historical period and how people used animal skin to make clothing.

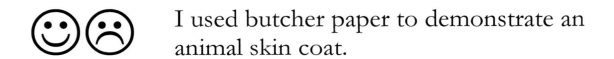 I used butcher paper to demonstrate an animal skin coat.

😊 ☹ I shared with the class about my animal skin coat.

😊 ☹ I displayed my animal skin coat.

Little House Social Studies Curriculum Guide ©2005

Teacher Scoring Guide

Title: **Lesson 6 - Replica of Animal Skin**

[4] Exemplary	
	o Clearly addresses devising an animal skin coat.
	o Cleverly designs an animal skin coat using butcher paper, markers and paint.
	o Fluently shares about using animal skin for clothing.
	o Effectively displays animal skin coat.

[3] Proficient	
	o Reasonably outlines an animal skin coat.
	o Appropriately creates an animal skin coat using butcher paper, markers and paint.
	o Generally outlines using animal skin for clothing.
	o Fairly strong display of animal skin coat.

[2] Apprentice	
	o Inconsistent explaining of an animal skin coat.
	o Too many missing aspects of depicting an animal skin coat using butcher paper, markers and paint.
	o Many errors generalizing about using animal skin for clothing.
	o Significant weakness in display of animal skin coat.

[1] Novice	
	o Unclear recall of an animal skin coat.
	o Serious errors making an animal skin coat using butcher paper, markers and paint.
	o Very little describing of using animal skin for clothing.
	o Incomplete display of animal skin coat.

Lesson Plan

Title:	**Lesson 7 - Indian Beads**

Date:		Grade:	K-4

Suggested Season / Date: Autumn / October, week 3

Time: 30 minutes (approx.)

Subject: Social Studies, Anthropology Activities

Learning Style / Different Multiple Intelligences: Tactile/Kinesthetic; Bodily Kinesthetic (activity could be used for all areas)

Example: hands on, touching, feeling and handling objects: beads, macaroni

Materials Needed:

1) *Little House on the Prairie*, pages 169-252
2) *Little House in the Classroom*, pages 49-53
3) *The World of Little House*, pages 25-32
4) *Across the Curriculum with Favorite Authors*, page 42
5) *Inside Laura's Little House*, pages 88-90
6) *My Little House Crafts Book*, pages 56-59
7) *Activities for Elementary School Social Studies*, pages 3.14-3.15 Adaptation
8) *Little House Social Studies Curriculum Guide*, Activity, Performance Assessment Task, Student Scoring Guide, Teacher Scoring Guide: Lesson 7 - Indian Beads

Introduction:

1) Read from *Little House on the Prairie*.
2) Discuss Osage Indians and their use of Indian beads.
3) The purpose is to learn about Laura's experience finding Indian beads and learning to design Indian jewelry with the beads.

Major Instructional Sequence:

4) Provide information about Osage life on the prairie and how Laura's family was part of that life.
5) Allow time for questions about the Osage use of beads.
6) Ask questions for understanding.

Concluding Sequence/Closure:

7) *Little House Social Studies Curriculum Guide*, Activity: Lesson 7 - Indian Beads

Evaluation:

8) *Little House Social Studies Curriculum Guide*, Performance Assessment Task, Student Scoring Guide, Teacher Scoring Guide: Lesson 7 - Indian Beads

Alignment to State Standards:

(compare to standards shown: Arkansas)

Strand 1:	Time, Continuity and Change
Content Standard 2:	Students will demonstrate an understanding of now ideas, events and conditions bring about change.

Learning Expectations

TCC.2.1	Discuss and record changes in one's self, community, state and nation.
TCC.2.2	Illustrate that change is inevitable and universal and affects everyone.
TCC.2.3	Use personal experiences, biographies or historical fiction to explain how individuals are affected by, can cope with and can create change.

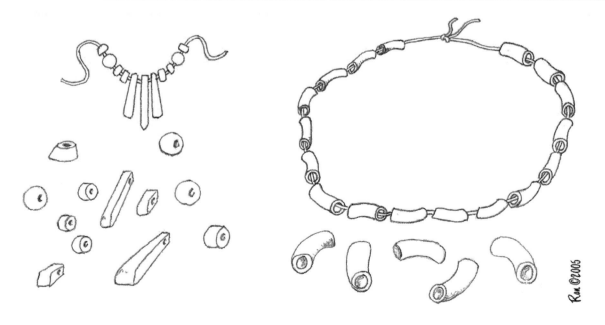

Activity

Title: **Lesson 7 - Indian Beads**

Sources:

1) *Activities for Elementary School Social Studies*, pages 3.14-3.15 Adaptation

Materials Needed:

1) colored macaroni (various shapes)
2) pipe cleaners
3) small containers (to put beads in)

Objectives:

As a result of this activity, the student will:
o make Native American bead jewelry
o develop an understanding and appreciation of the use of beads in Native American jewelry and clothing, moccasins

Introduction:

1) Pass model bead jewelry around for students to examine.
2) Discuss the use and importance of bead jewelry for Native Americans.
3) Tell students they will make their own Native American bead jewelry.

Major Instructional Sequence:

4) Have students obtain the necessary materials from the work area.
5) Demonstrate the steps in making the bead jewelry.
6) Circulate as students construct Indian jewelry, check for understanding and give assistance when needed.

Concluding Sequence/Closure:

7) Each student shows and describes their Indian bead jewelry.
8) Make a display of the Native American bead jewelry.

Performance Assessment Task

Title:	**Lesson 7 - Indian Beads**		

Name:		Grade:	K-4
Date:		Subject:	Social Studies

Alignment to State Standards:
(minimum of three standards, input State standards below)

Code	Standard Description

Description of Performance Task:
(include time, student performance, assessment)

Time:	30 minutes (approx.)
Activity:	Activity will correlate with reading *Little House on the Prairie*.
Task:	o Student will name use of Indian beads for jewelry, clothing, moccasins. o Student will discuss an appreciation of beads in Indian jewelry. o Student will discover a variety of ways to string macaroni on pipe cleaners. o Student will design the Indian jewelry using colored macaroni and pipe cleaners. o Student will model the Indian bead jewelry. o Student will display the Indian bead jewelry.

Student Scoring Guide: | (attach a copy) |

Teacher Scoring Guide: | (attach a copy of scoring key) |
Score (select one): | [4] Exemplary [3] Proficient [2] Apprentice [1] Novice |

Student Scoring Guide

Title: **Lesson 7 - Indian Beads**

Name:

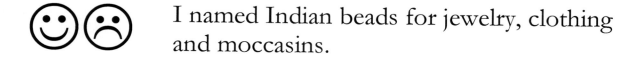 I named Indian beads for jewelry, clothing and moccasins.

I discussed an appreciation of the use of beads in Indian jewelry.

I discovered a variety of ways to string macaroni on pipe cleaners.

I designed my Indian jewelry using colored macaroni and pipe cleaners.

I modeled my Indian jewelry.

Little House Social Studies Curriculum Guide ©2005

Teacher Scoring Guide

Title: | **Lesson 7 - Indian Beads**

---

[4] Exemplary
- Effectively summarizes Indian beads for jewelry, clothing and moccasins.
- Clearly addresses ways to string macaroni on pipe cleaners.
- Consistently combines macaroni on pipe cleaners to design Indian jewelry.
- Contains few errors modeling and displaying Indian jewelry.

---

[3] Proficient
- Fairly strongly differentiates Indian beads for jewelry, clothing and moccasins.
- Progressive solution of ways to string macaroni on pipe cleaners.
- Appropriately uses macaroni on pipe cleaners to design Indian jewelry.
- Reasonably models and displays Indian jewelry.

---

[2] Apprentice
- Inconsistently discusses Indian beads for jewelry, clothing and moccasins.
- Distracting estimate of ways to string macaroni on pipe cleaners.
- Not too clear in use of macaroni on pipe cleaners to design Indian jewelry.
- Not much information modeling and displaying Indian jewelry.

---

[1] Novice
- Little or no naming of Indian beads for jewelry, clothing and moccasins.
- Very little defining of ways to string macaroni on pipe cleaners.
- Serious errors in identifying macaroni on pipe cleaners to design Indian jewelry.
- Lacks modeling and displaying Indian jewelry.

Lesson Plan

Title:	**Lesson 8 - Native American Rainstick**

Date:		Grade:	K-4

Suggested Season / Date: Autumn / October, week 4

Time: 30 minutes (approx.)

Subject: Social Studies, Anthropology Activities

Learning Style / Different Multiple Intelligences: Tactile/Kinesthetic; Musical/Rhythmic Intelligences (activity could be used for all areas)

Example: hands on, moving, doing, touching, play an instrument and respond to music

Materials Needed:

1) *Little House on the Prairie*, pages 253-335
2) *Across the Curriculum with Favorite Authors*, page 43
3) *Inside Laura's Little House*, pages 80-85
4) *Little House in the Classroom*, pages 49-54
5) *Activities for Elementary School Social Studies*, pages 3.17-3.18 Adaptation
6) *Little House Social Studies Curriculum Guide*, Activity, Performance Assessment Task, Student Scoring Guide, Teacher Scoring Guide: Lesson 8 - Native American Rainstick

Introduction:

1) Read from *Little House on the Prairie*.
2) The purpose is to design a replica of a Native American rainstick.

Major Instructional Sequence:

3) Provide information about Osage Indian music and dancing.

Little House Social Studies Curriculum Guide ©2005

4) Provide examples and pictures of Indian music.
5) Discussion and check for understanding.

Concluding Sequence/Closure:

6) *Little House Social Studies Curriculum Guide*, Activity: Lesson 8 - Native American Rainstick

Evaluation:

7) *Little House Social Studies Curriculum Guide*, Performance Assessment Task, Student Scoring Guide, Teacher Scoring Guide: Lesson 8 - Native American Rainstick

Alignment to State Standards:

(compare to standards shown: Arkansas)

Strand 2:	People, Places and Environments
Content Standard 1:	Students will demonstrate an understanding that people, cultures and systems are connected and that commonalities and diversities exist among them.

Learning Expectations

PPE.1.2	Compare and contrast similarities and differences in cultures through a variety of experiences, such as reading, writing, drawing, role-playing, dance, music and simulation.
PPE.1.4	Use student, family and community resources to recognize and understand the ethnic, racial and religious diversity of the United States.
PPE.1.6	Distinguish similarities and differences among families and communities around the world.

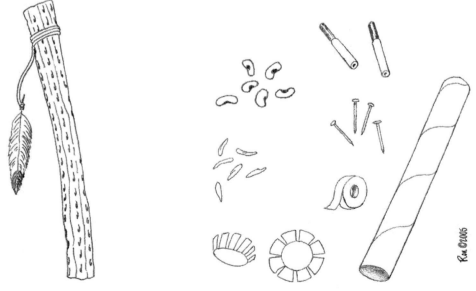

Activity

Title: **Lesson 8 - Native American Rainstick**

Sources:

1) *Activities for Elementary School Social Studies*, pages 3.17-3.18 Adaptation

Materials Needed:

1) large paper towel rolls
2) construction paper, markers and tape
3) seeds, beans and rice
4) a sample rainstick

Objectives:

As a result of this activity, the student will:
o produce a replica of a Native American rainstick
o decorate the rainstick with Native American design
o demonstrate the use of the rainstick to make sounds

Introduction:

1) Show a model of a sample rainstick and demonstrate its sounds.
2) Let students examine the rainstick and move it to make sounds.
3) Relate how tribes in America use the rainstick to simulate the sound of rain.
4) Tell students that they will make their own Native American rainstick.

Major Instructional Sequence:

5) Assemble groups at work stations where the materials are available.
6) Cover one end of the towel roll, reinforce with tape and put rice, beans and seeds in the tube.
7) Use construction paper, markers for American Indian designs.

Concluding Sequence/Closure:

8) Have students show their rainsticks and share about their designs.
9) Place the rainsticks in a classroom exhibit.

Performance Assessment Task

Title: | **Lesson 8 - Native American Rainstick**

Name: | Grade: | K-4

Date: | Subject: | Social Studies

Alignment to State Standards:
(minimum of three standards, input State standards below)

Code	Standard Description

Description of Performance Task:
(include time, student performance, assessment)

Time: | 30 minutes (approx.)

Activity: | Activity will correlate with reading *Little House on the Prairie*.

Task:
- o Student will describe a Native American rainstick.
- o Student will discuss how the rainstick was used to simulate the sound of rain.
- o Student will produce a replica of a Native American rainstick using rice, beans and seeds inside a paper towel roll to apply the sound of rain.
- o Student will decorate the rainstick using Native American design.
- o Student will demonstrate and exhibit the rainstick.

Student Scoring Guide: | (attach a copy)

Teacher Scoring Guide: | (attach a copy of scoring key)
Score (select one): | [4] Exemplary [3] Proficient [2] Apprentice [1] Novice

Student Scoring Guide

Title: **Lesson 8 - Native American Rainstick**

Name:

 I described a Native American rainstick.

☺☹ I discussed how the rainstick was used to simulate the sound of rain.

☺☹ I used rice, beans and seeds inside the rainstick to create the sound of rain.

☺☹ I decorated my rainstick using a Native American design.

☺☹ I exhibited my Native American rainstick.

Little House Social Studies Curriculum Guide ©2005

Teacher Scoring Guide

Title:	Lesson 8 - Native American Rainstick

[4] Exemplary	<ul><li>Effective description of a Native American rainstick.</li><li>Combines and compiles rice, beans and seeds inside the rainstick to simulate the sound of rain.</li><li>Using variety interprets the Native American design.</li><li>Handles well an exhibit of Native American rainstick.</li></ul>
[3] Proficient	<ul><li>Fairly strong depiction of a Native American rainstick.</li><li>Clear use of rice, beans and seeds inside the rainstick to simulate the sound of rain.</li><li>Appropriately decorates the Native American design.</li><li>Reasonably devises an exhibit of Native American rainstick.</li></ul>
[2] Apprentice	<ul><li>Inconsistent explanation of a Native American rainstick.</li><li>Significant weakness using rice, beans and seeds inside the rainstick to simulate the sound of rain.</li><li>Inappropriate inference of the Native American design.</li><li>Too many missing extensions in exhibit of Native American rainstick.</li></ul>
[1] Novice	<ul><li>Lack evidence of naming a Native American rainstick.</li><li>Very little use of rice, beans and seeds inside the rainstick to simulate the sound of rain.</li><li>Serious errors identifying the Native American design.</li><li>Little or no exhibition of Native American rainstick.</li></ul>

Lesson Plan

Title:	**Lesson 9 - Practice Voting**

Date:		Grade:	K-4

Suggested Season / Date: | Autumn / November, week 1

Time: | 30 minutes (approx.)

Subject: | Social Studies, Political Science Activities

Learning Style / Different Multiple Intelligences: | Tactile/Kinesthetic; Logical/Mathematical Intelligences (activity could be used for all areas)

Example: | hands on, doing and touching, counting ballots

Materials Needed:

1) *Farmer Boy*, pages 1-93
2) *The World of Little House*, pages 38-41
3) *Across the Curriculum with Favorite Authors*, pages 27-28
4) *Activities for Elementary School Social Studies*, pages 6.6-6.7 Adaptation
5) *Little House Social Studies Curriculum Guide*, Activity, Performance Assessment Task, Student Scoring Guide, Teacher Scoring Guide: Lesson 9 - Practice Voting

Introduction:

1) Read from *Farmer Boy*.
2) Explain the need for rules and depict the process of voting.
3) The purpose is to understand the significance of voting.

Major Instructional Sequence:

4) Provide information about voting.

Little House Social Studies Curriculum Guide ©2005

5) Give instruction and discuss the voting process.
6) Check for understanding.

Concluding Sequence/Closure:

7) *Little House Social Studies Curriculum Guide*, Activity: Lesson 9 - Practice Voting

Evaluation:

8) *Little House Social Studies Curriculum Guide*, Performance Assessment Task, Student Scoring Guide, Teacher Scoring Guide: Lesson 9 - Practice Voting

Alignment to State Standards:

(compare to standards shown: Arkansas)

Strand 4:	Power, Authority and Governance
Content Standard 2:	Students will demonstrate an understanding of the commonalities and differences of various systems of government.

Learning Expectations

PAG.2.1	Explain why government is necessary in classroom, school, community, state and nation.
PAG.2.2	Distinguish among school, community, state and national governments and identify leaders at these levels, such as superintendent, mayor, governor and president.
PAG.2.3	Identify services provided by community, state and national governments.

Activity

Title: | **Lesson 9 - Practice Voting**

Sources:

1) *Activities for Elementary School Social Studies*, pages 6.6-6.7 Adaptation

Materials Needed:

1) cardboard box
2) 3" x 5" index cards
3) marking pens

Objectives:

As a result of this activity, the student will:
o use voting to make individual decisions
o vote on specific issues as a class
o work cooperatively to count ballots from ballot box

Introduction:

1) Lead class to the conclusion that voting is the democratic process used by groups to make group decisions. Emphasize that voting is usually done by secret ballot. Talk about school to national elections as examples.
2) Tell the class they will vote by secret ballot and will participate in elections to make decisions (practice).

Major Instructional Sequence:

3) Students will design a ballot box.
4) Student will vote on index cards with marking pens.
5) Students will count ballots at the end of the voting process.
6) A chart will be helpful in tabulating the votes for each student.

Concluding Sequence/Closure:

7) Students will announce results.
8) Chart will be displayed on bulletin board.

Little House Social Studies Curriculum Guide ©2005

Performance Assessment Task

Title: **Lesson 9 - Practice Voting**

Name:

Date:

Grade: K-4

Subject: Social Studies

Alignment to State Standards:
(minimum of three standards, input State standards below)

Code	Standard Description

Description of Performance Task:
(include time, student performance, assessment)

Time:	30 minutes (approx.)
Activity:	Activity will correlate with reading *Farmer Boy*.
Task:	o Student will recite information about the democratic process.
	o Student will summarize about voting for elections.
	o Student will design ballot box.
	o Student will vote on index card using marking pen.
	o Student will count the ballots from the ballot box.
	o Student will interpret and chart the tabulated votes.

Student Scoring Guide: (attach a copy)

Teacher Scoring Guide: (attach a copy of scoring key)

Score (select one): [4] Exemplary [3] Proficient [2] Apprentice [1] Novice

Student Scoring Guide

Title: **Lesson 9 - Practice Voting**

Name:

 I recited information about the democratic process.

 I summarized about voting in the election process.

 I used boxes, index cards and marking pens for the voting process.

 I voted, along with the class, on an index card with a marking pen.

 I interpreted the results, along with the class, and charted the tabulated votes.

Little House Social Studies Curriculum Guide ©2005

Teacher Scoring Guide

Title: | **Lesson 9 - Practice Voting**

[4] Exemplary
- o Fluently appraises the democratic process.
- o Contains few errors justifying use of boxes, index cards and marking pens for the voting process.
- o Handles well formulating the voting process.
- o Appropriately tabulates and charts the votes in a display.

[3] Proficient
- o Fairly strongly deduces the democratic process.
- o Generally uses boxes, index cards and marking pens for the voting process.
- o Reasonably relates the voting process.
- o Some weakness interpreting the votes in a display.

[2] Apprentice
- o Inconsistent defining of the democratic process.
- o Not focusing on using boxes, index cards and marking pen for the voting process.
- o Contains some sense of the voting process.
- o Significant weakness recalling the votes in a display.

[1] Novice
- o Little or no naming of the democratic process.
- o Lacks general use of boxes, index cards and marking pens for the voting process.
- o Serious errors in identifying the voting process.
- o Impeded results of the votes in a display.

Lesson Plan

Title:	**Lesson 10 - Independence Day**

Date:		Grade:	K-4

Suggested Season / Date: Autumn / November, week 2

Time: 30 minutes (approx.)

Subject: Social Studies, History Activities

Learning Style / Different Multiple Intelligences: Visual; Visual/Spatial Intelligences (activity could be used for all areas)

Example: seeing visuals, pictures, slides, filmstrips, videos and drawing

Materials Needed:

1) *Farmer Boy*, pages 94-186
2) *The World of Little House*, pages 43-45
3) *Across the Curriculum with Favorite Authors*, page 30
4) *Activities for Elementary School Social Studies*, pages 2.10-2.11
5) *Little House Social Studies Curriculum Guide*, Activity, Performance Assessment Task, Student Scoring Guide, Teacher Scoring Guide: Lesson 10 - Independence Day

Introduction:

1) Read from *Farmer Boy*.
2) Use reference materials such as picture, slides or filmstrip depicting Independence Day.
3) The purpose is to understand the significance of Independence Day.

Major Instructional Sequence:

4) Provide information about Independence Day.
5) Give instruction and discuss about Independence Day.

Little House Social Studies Curriculum Guide ©2005

6) Check for understanding.

Concluding Sequence/Closure:

7) *Little House Social Studies Curriculum Guide*, Activity: Lesson 10 - Independence Day

Evaluation:

8) *Little House Social Studies Curriculum Guide*, Performance Assessment Task, Student Scoring Guide, Teacher Scoring Guide: Lesson 10 - Independence Day

Alignment to State Standards:

(compare to standards shown: Arkansas)

Strand 4:	Power, Authority and Governance
Content Standard 1:	Students will demonstrate an understanding of the ideals, right and responsibilities of participating in democratic society.

Learning Expectations

PAG.1.3	Illustrate ways that current events may influence people's lives.
PAG.1.4	Describe the basic structure of the United States government.
PAG.1.5	Discuss the five basic freedoms (speech, religion, press, assembly and petition) guaranteed to all United States citizens.

Activity

Title: **Lesson 10 - Independence Day**

Sources:

1) *Activities for Elementary School Social Studies*, pages 2.10-2.11

Materials Needed:

1) drawing paper, pencils, crayons, coloring pencils
2) informational books, history books and reference materials such as pictured encyclopedias and picture dictionaries
3) pictures, slides or videos depicting Independence Day

Objectives:

As a result of this activity, the student will:
o understand the significance of the Fourth of July in America
o produce an original drawing depicting a Fourth of July activity

Introduction:

1) Use the following background information to give students a short overview of Independence Day in America:

> **Independence Day**
> "The most important national holiday in the United States is Independence Day, July 4, which celebrates the adoption of the Declaration of Independence by the Second Continental Congress on July 4, 1776. The day always has picnics and every variety of noisy jubilation. In fact, the firing of cannon and fireworks caused so many injuries that, by the early 1900's, ordinances forbidding private fireworks were passed in many cities. Today, Fourth of July fireworks are largely handled by professionals." (Stockard)

Major Instructional Sequence:

2) Have students use reference materials to find as much information as possible about Independence Day in America.
3) Students are to draw an original Fourth of July scene on the art paper.
4) Circulate, check for understanding and give assistance when needed.

Concluding Sequence/Closure:

5) Students show and tell about their drawing.
6) Place the drawings on the bulletin board.

Performance Assessment Task

Title: **Lesson 10 - Independence Day**

Name:

Date:

Grade: K-4

Subject: Social Studies

Alignment to State Standards:
(minimum of three standards, input State standards below)

Code	Standard Description

Description of Performance Task:
(include time, student performance, assessment)

Time: 30 minutes (approx.)

Activity: Activity will correlate with reading *Farmer Boy*.

Task:
- o Student will define what the Fourth of July is.
- o Student will investigate using reference materials to find information about Independence Day.
- o Student will illustrate an original Fourth of July scene on the art paper.
- o Student will share about the Fourth of July scene.
- o Drawing will be exhibited on the bulletin board.

Student Scoring Guide: (attach a copy)

Teacher Scoring Guide: (attach a copy of scoring key)

Score (select one): [4] Exemplary [3] Proficient [2] Apprentice [1] Novice

Student Scoring Guide

Title: **Lesson 10 - Independence Day**

Name:

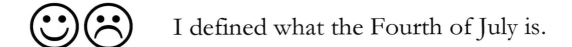 I defined what the Fourth of July is.

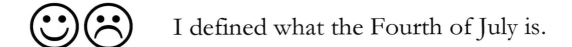 I investigated using reference materials to find more information.

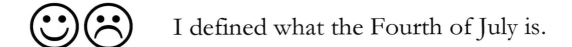 I illustrated by using drawing paper and pens.

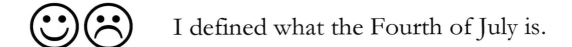 I shared about my Fourth of July scene.

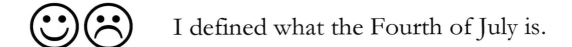 I exhibited my drawing on the bulletin board.

Teacher Scoring Guide

Title: | **Lesson 10 - Independence Day**

---

[4] Exemplary
- Fluently contrasts what the Fourth of July is.
- Develops and compiles information through use of reference materials.
- Excellent sharing the Fourth of July on drawing paper.
- Clever display of drawing on the bulletin board.

---

[3] Proficient
- Appropriately differentiates what the Fourth of July is.
- Clearly illustrates information through use of reference materials.
- Reasonably shares the Fourth of July on drawing paper.
- Fairly strong exhibit of drawing on the bulletin board.

---

[2] Apprentice
- Inconsistently explains what the Fourth of July is.
- Many errors explaining information through use of reference materials.
- Not clear summarizing the Fourth of July on drawing paper.
- Significant weakness labeling of drawing on the bulletin board.

---

[1] Novice
- Very little naming of what the Fourth of July is.
- Serious errors selecting information through use of reference materials.
- Lacks stating the Fourth of July on drawing paper.
- Unclear labeling of drawing on the bulletin board.

Lesson Plan

Title:	**Lesson 11 - Coalescing (Making Butter)**

Date:		Grade:	K-4

Suggested Season / Date: | Autumn / November, week 3

Time: | 30 minutes (approx.)

Subject: | Social Studies, Anthropology Activities

Learning Style / Different Multiple Intelligences: | Tactile/Kinesthetic; Bodily/Kinesthetic Intelligence (activity could be used for all areas)

Example: | hands on, moving, handling crafts skillfully, interact with space and processing knowledge of movement to make butter

Materials Needed:

1) *Farmer Boy*, pages 187-279
2) *The Little House Cookbook*, pages 166-169
3) *The World of Little House*, page 47
4) *Across the Curriculum with Favorite Authors*, pages 21, 30
5) *Activities for Elementary School Social Studies*, page 3.16 Adaptation
6) *Little House Social Studies Curriculum Guide*, Activity, Performance Assessment Task, Student Scoring Guide, Teacher Scoring Guide: Lesson 11 - Coalescing (Making Butter)

Introduction:

1) Read from *Farmer Boy*.
2) Share information about making butter.
3) The purpose is to learn about making butter.

Major Instructional Sequence:

4) Discuss to appreciate the effort of making and selling quality butter. Compare to ease of buying butter today.

5) Explain concept of coalescing (making butter).

6) Ask questions about coalescing (making butter).

Concluding Sequence/Closure:

7) *Little House Social Studies Curriculum Guide*, Activity: Lesson 11 - Coalescing (Making Butter)

Evaluation:

8) *Little House Social Studies Curriculum Guide*, Performance Assessment Task, Student Scoring Guide, Teacher Scoring Guide: Lesson 11 - Coalescing (Making Butter)

Alignment to State Standards:

(compare to standards shown: Arkansas)

Strand 2:	People, Places and Environments
Content Standard 1:	Students will demonstrate an understanding that people, cultures and systems are connected and that commonalities and diversities exist among them.

Learning Expectations

PPE.1.1	Investigate how members of a family, school, community, state, nation and culture depend on each other.
PPE.1.3	Analyze the contributions of various groups to community, state and nation.
PPE.1.5	Analyze the effects of interactions between people and their environment.

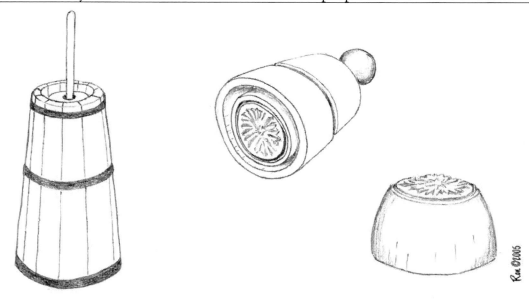

Activity

Title: | **Lesson 11 - Coalescing (Making Butter)**

Sources:

1) *Activities for Elementary School Social Studies*, page 3.16 Adaptation

Materials Needed:

1) ½ pint whipping cream
2) 1 pint canning jar and lid
3) marble
4) small tub and knife
5) crackers or bread

Objectives:

As a result of this activity, the student will:
o produce a mold of butter
o produce buttermilk
o examine butter through touch, smell and taste
o understand and appreciate the effort of making butter

Introduction:

1) Lead a discussion of the importance of making butter.
2) Tell students they will make their own butter.

Major Instructional Sequence:

3) Demonstrate how to shake the jar for coalescing (making butter).
4) Let each student shake the jar until the coalescing takes place, forming the lump of butter and buttermilk.
5) Once students have made the butter, each will sample the butter on crackers or bread.

Concluding Sequence/Closure:

6) Each student will describe about shaking the jar; making butter.
7) Lead in discussion of how the butter tasted on cracker or bread.

Little House Social Studies Curriculum Guide ©2005

Performance Assessment Task

Title: **Lesson 11 - Coalescing (Making Butter)**

Name:

Date:

Grade: K-4

Subject: Social Studies

Alignment to State Standards:
(minimum of three standards, input State standards below)

Code	Standard Description

Description of Performance Task:
(include time, student performance, assessment)

Time: 30 minutes (approx.)

Activity: Activity will correlate with reading *Farmer Boy*.

Task:
- o Student will identify the process of coalescing (making butter).
- o Student will investigate information about the process of making butter.
- o Student will demonstrate shaking jar of whipping cream with marble inside.
- o Student will observe the coalescing process.
- o Student will press the lump in to the butter mold.
- o Student will touch, smell and taste real butter on bread or cracker.
- o Student will share about the process of coalescing (making butter).

Student Scoring Guide: (attach a copy)

Teacher Scoring Guide: (attach a copy of scoring key)

Score (select one): [4] Exemplary [3] Proficient [2] Apprentice [1] Novice

Student Scoring Guide

Title: | **Lesson 11 - Coalescing (Making Butter)**

Name:

☺ ☹ I identified the process of coalescing (making butter).

☺ ☹ I investigated information about the process of making butter.

☺ ☹ I demonstrated the process by shaking the jar of whipping cream with a marble and then pressing it in to the butter mold.

☺ ☹ I analyzed the butter by tasting the butter on bread.

☺ ☹ I shared about the process of coalescing (making butter).

Little House Social Studies Curriculum Guide ©2005

Teacher Scoring Guide

Title: | **Lesson 11 - Coalescing (Making Butter)**

[4] Exemplary	o Effectively concludes about the process of coalescing (making butter).
	o Consistently validates the process by shaking the whipping cream in the jar.
	o Genuinely concludes process by sampling butter on bread or cracker.
	o Fluently shares about coalescing (making butter).

[3] Proficient	o Clearly differentiates the process of coalescing (making butter).
	o Appropriately demonstrates the process by shaking the whipping cream in the jar.
	o Reasonably prepares process by sampling butter on bread or cracker.
	o Some errors relating about coalescing (making butter).

[2] Apprentice	o No particular order of explaining the process of coalescing (making butter).
	o Weak progression of predicting the process by shaking the whipping cream in the jar.
	o Inconsistently summarizes process by sampling butter on bread or cracker.
	o Many errors in paraphrasing about coalescing (making butter).

[1] Novice	o Unclear in defining of process of coalescing (making butter).
	o Little or no labeling of the process by shaking the whipping cream in the jar.
	o Little or no identification of process by sampling butter on bread or cracker.
	o Incomplete naming of coalescing (making butter).

Lesson Plan

Title:	**Lesson 12 - Candle-Making**

Date:		Grade:	K-4

Suggested Season / Date: | Autumn / November, week 4

Time: | 30 minutes (approx.)

Subject: | Social Studies, History Activities

Learning Style / Different Multiple Intelligences: | Tactile/Kinesthetic; Visual/Spatial Intelligences (activity could be used for all areas)

Example: | hands on, doing, touching, building, creating and making a candle

Materials Needed:

1) *Farmer Boy*, pages 280-372
2) *Across the Curriculum with Favorite Authors*, pages 31, 38
3) *Activities for Elementary School Social Studies*, page 2.5
4) *Little House Social Studies Curriculum Guide*, Activity, Performance Assessment Task, Student Scoring Guide, Teacher Scoring Guide: Lesson 12 - Candle-Making

Introduction:

1) Read from *Farmer Boy*.
2) Show a few candles of different types, pass around and examine.
3) Discuss what candles might be used for.
4) The purpose is to learn about making candles.

Major Instructional Sequence:

5) Display candles and examine them. Discuss differences between using light bulbs now and candles in Laura's day. Explain concept of candle-making.

6) Model candle-making. Allow time for questions about process.
7) Ask students questions for understanding and make explanations.

Concluding Sequence/Closure:

8) *Little House Social Studies Curriculum Guide*, Activity: Lesson 12 - Candle-Making

Evaluation:

9) *Little House Social Studies Curriculum Guide*, Performance Assessment Task, Student Scoring Guide, Teacher Scoring Guide: Lesson 12 - Candle-Making

Alignment to State Standards:

(compare to standards shown: Arkansas)

Strand 1:	Time, Continuity and Change
Content Standard 1:	Students will demonstrate an understanding of the chronology and concepts of history and identify and explain historical relationships.

Learning Expectations

TCC.1.1	Examine and analyze stories of important Americans and their contributions to our society.
TCC.1.4	Describe how history is a continuing story of events, people and places.
TCC.1.7	Use literature and the arts to show how people, places and events are connected to the past.

Activity

Title:

Lesson 12 - Candle-Making

Sources:

1) *Activities for Elementary School Social Studies*, page 2.5

Materials Needed:

1) pencils and scissors
2) pieces of string (approximately 6" long)
3) empty egg cartons
4) paraffin wax
5) metal cooking pot (about one quart size)
6) electric burner

Objectives:

As a result of this activity, the student will:
o produce a candle
o understand and appreciate how people functioned before electricity was available

Introduction:

1) Show the students candles of different types.
2) Let students pass the candles around and examine them. Discuss what candles might be used for.
3) Discuss how candles were used for light before electric light bulbs were invented.

Major Instructional Sequence:

4) Teacher will model process of candle-making.
5) Student will observe adult (parent) candle-making and participate with adult (parent) supervision.

Concluding Sequence/Closure:

6) Each student will show and tell about their candle.
7) Each student will display their candle.

Performance Assessment Task

Title: | **Lesson 12 - Candle-Making**

Name: | | Grade: | K-4
Date: | | Subject: | Social Studies

Alignment to State Standards:
(minimum of three standards, input State standards below)

Code	Standard Description

Description of Performance Task:
(include time, student performance, assessment)

Time: | 30 minutes (approx.)
Activity: | Activity will correlate with reading *Farmer Boy*.
Task: | o Student will describe candles of different types.
 | o Student will discuss what candles might be used for in Laura's day.
 | o Student will use paraffin wax and string (teacher/parent assisted) to demonstrate candle-making.
 | o Student will create a candle.
 | o Student will display the candle.

Student Scoring Guide: | (attach a copy)

Teacher Scoring Guide: | (attach a copy of scoring key)
Score (select one): | [4] Exemplary [3] Proficient [2] Apprentice [1] Novice

Student Scoring Guide

Title: | **Lesson 12 - Candle-Making**

Name:

😊😞 I described candles of different types.

😊😞 I discussed what candles might be used for.

😊😞 I used paraffin wax and string to demonstrate candle-making.

😊😞 I created a candle.

😊😞 I displayed my candle.

Teacher Scoring Guide

Title: **Lesson 12 - Candle-Making**

[4] Exemplary	o Fluently categorized different types of candles.
	o Effectively appraised what candles might be used for.
	o Handled well composing paraffin wax and string into a candle.
	o Appropriately display of a candle.

[3] Proficient	o Ideas progress relating to different types of candles.
	o Clearly deduces what candles might be used for.
	o Focuses on developing paraffin wax and string into a candle.
	o Fairly strong display of a candle.

[2] Apprentice	o Not too clear explaining different types of candles.
	o Not focused in generalizing what candles might be used for.
	o Inconsistent converting paraffin wax and string into candle.
	o Significant weakness in displaying a candle.

[1] Novice	o Lacks evidence of defining different types of candles.
	o Difficult to follow discussing what candles might be used for.
	o Serious errors changing paraffin was and string into candle.
	o Little or no display of a candle.

Lesson Plan

Title:	**Lesson 13 - Locating the State**

Date:		Grade:	K-4

Suggested Season / Date:	Winter / December, week 1

Time:	30 minutes (approx.)

Subject:	Social Studies, Geography Activities

Learning Style / Different Multiple Intelligences:	Visual; Visual/Spatial Intelligences (activity could be used for all areas)

Example:	seeing maps, charts, pictures, hand outs and create map

Materials Needed:

1) *On the Banks of Plum Creek*, pages 1-85
2) *The World of Little House*, pages 50-54
3) *Little House in the Classroom*, pages 56-59 (maps pages 22, 59)
4) *Across the Curriculum with Favorite Authors*, pages 52-53
5) *Activities for Elementary School Social Studies*, pages 1.30-1.31 Adaptation
6) *Little House Social Studies Curriculum Guide*, Activity, Performance Assessment Task, Student Scoring Guide, Teacher Scoring Guide: Lesson 13 - Locating the State

Introduction:

1) Read from *On the Banks of Plum Creek*.
2) Share information from sources about where Laura lived.
3) The purpose is to understand about the state where Laura and her family lived.

Major Instructional Sequence:

4) Provide information and explain concepts about the state where Laura and her family lived. State definitions needed.

Little House Social Studies Curriculum Guide ©2005

5) Provide examples of the state. Discuss and check for understanding.
6) Pose key questions about Minnesota (ask students to explain attributes in their own words).

Concluding Sequence/Closure:

7) *Little House Social Studies Curriculum Guide*, Activity: Lesson 13 - Locating the State

Evaluation:

8) *Little House Social Studies Curriculum Guide*, Performance Assessment Task, Student Scoring Guide, Teacher Scoring Guide: Lesson 13 - Locating the State

Alignment to State Standards:

(compare to standards shown: Arkansas)

Strand 2:	People, Places and Environments
Content Standard 2:	Students will demonstrate an understanding of the significance of physical and cultural characteristics of places and world regions.

Learning Expectations

PPE.2.2	Understand and apply the five themes of geography: location, place, human-environment interaction, movement and regions.
PPE.2.4	Understand the various types of maps and uses.
PPE.2.5	Understand geographical terms such as, mental mapping, spatial relationships, cardinal directions, landforms.

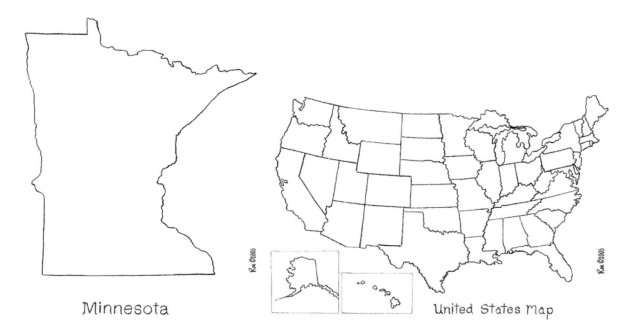

Minnesota   United States Map

Activity

| Title: | **Lesson 13 - Locating the State** |

Sources:

1) *Activities for Elementary School Social Studies*, pages 1.30-1.31 Adaptation

Materials Needed:

1) coloring maps of Minnesota (see Activity Worksheets at the end of this guide)
2) coloring maps of United States (see Activity Worksheets at the end of this guide)
3) crayons/colored pencils

Objectives:

As a result of this activity, the student will:
o develop an understanding where Minnesota is in relation to [your home state]
o learn where the Ingalls traveled
o visually see where the Ingalls lived
o compare the state of Minnesota with [your home state]

Introduction:

1) Using the United States map, point out where Minnesota and [your home state] are located.
2) Point out the objective is to learn where the Ingalls traveled and lived in relation to [your home state].

Major Instructional Sequence:

3) Pass out a copy of the United States and Minnesota map.
4) Direct students to listen carefully and follow instructions:
   o Color Minnesota the same color on both pages.
   o Color [your home state] another color.
   o Color the states around them using a third color.
   o Color the rest of the states a color they choose.
5) Create a key telling what the colors mean.

Concluding Sequence/Closure:

6) Let each student show and tell about their map.
7) Display maps in the classroom.

Little House Social Studies Curriculum Guide ©2005

Performance Assessment Task

Title: **Lesson 13 - Locating the State**

Name:

Date:

Grade: K-4

Subject: Social Studies

Alignment to State Standards:
(minimum of three standards, input State standards below)

Code	Standard Description

Description of Performance Task:
(include time, student performance, assessment)

Time: 30 minutes (approx.)

Activity: Activity will correlate with reading *On the Banks of Plum Creek*.

Task:
- o Student will identify where Laura lived in Minnesota.
- o Student will observe where Minnesota is in relation to [your home state] and other states.
- o Student will color Minnesota on both maps, using the same color.
- o Student will use a second color for [your home state] and a third color for surrounding states.
- o Student will complete by coloring the other United States.
- o Student will create a color key to go with their map.
- o Student will display the United States map.

Student Scoring Guide: (attach a copy)

Teacher Scoring Guide: (attach a copy of scoring key)

Score (select one): [4] Exemplary [3] Proficient [2] Apprentice [1] Novice

Student Scoring Guide

Title: | **Lesson 13 - Locating the State**

Name: |

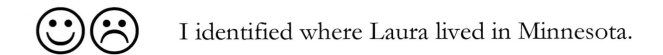 I identified where Laura lived in Minnesota.

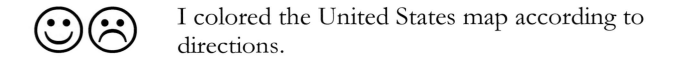 I observed where Minnesota is in relation to [your home state] and other states.

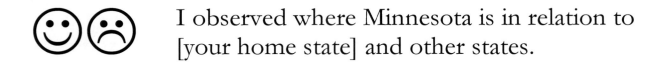 I colored the United States map according to directions.

I created a color key interpreting what the colors mean.

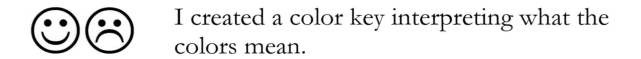 I displayed my United States map.

Teacher Scoring Guide

Title: **Lesson 13 - Locating the State**

[4] Exemplary	o Handles well formulating where Laura lived in Minnesota. o Develops and categorizes where Minnesota is in relation to [your home state] and other states. o Clearly addresses and compiles correct coloring to the various states. o Effectively designs states on a display of maps.
[3] Proficient	o Appropriately locates where Laura lived in Minnesota. o Differentiates where Minnesota is in relation to [your home state] and other states. o Some weakness producing correct coloring to the various states. o Some errors devising states on a display of maps.
[2] Apprentice	o Not much information explaining where Laura lived in Minnesota. o Not clear discriminating where Minnesota is in relation to [your home state] and other states. o Inconsistent distinguishing correct coloring to the various states. o Significant weakness selecting states on a display of maps.
[1] Novice	o Little or no naming of where Laura lived in Minnesota. o Lacks selecting where Minnesota is in relation to [your home state] and other states. o Very little matching correct coloring to the various states. o Unclear identification of states on a display of maps.

Lesson Plan

Title:	**Lesson 14 - Button String**

Date:		Grade:	K-4

Suggested Season / Date: Winter / December, week 2

Time: 30 minutes (approx.)

Subject: Social Studies, Anthropology Activities

Learning Style / Different Multiple Intelligences: Tactile/Kinesthetic; Visual/Spatial Intelligences (activity could be used for all areas)

Example: hands on, doing and touching, create and design button string

Materials Needed:

1) *On the Banks of Plum Creek*, pages 86-170
2) *My Little House Crafts Book*, pages 30-31
3) *Across the Curriculum with Favorite Authors*, pages 53, 59
4) *Activities for Elementary School Social Studies*, pages 3.10-3.11 Adaptation
5) *Little House Social Studies Curriculum Guide*, Activity, Performance Assessment Task, Student Scoring Guide, Teacher Scoring Guide: Lesson 14 - Button String

Introduction:

1) Read from *On the Banks of Plum Creek*.
2) Show different varieties of buttons.
3) The purpose is to learn to make a button string.

Major Instructional Sequence:

4) Show old and new buttons. Discuss how women kept buttons through generations in a button box. Explain concept of keeping unused buttons for making a button string.

Little House Social Studies Curriculum Guide ©2005

5) Model making a button string by threading buttons with heavy thread.
6) Check for understanding.

Concluding Sequence/Closure:

7) *Little House Social Studies Curriculum Guide*, Activity: Lesson 14 - Button String

Evaluation:

8) *Little House Social Studies Curriculum Guide*, Performance Assessment Task, Student Scoring Guide, Teacher Scoring Guide: Lesson 14 - Button String

Alignment to State Standards:

(compare to standards shown: Arkansas)

Strand 1:	Time, Continuity and Change
Content Standard 1:	Students will demonstrate an understanding of the chronology and concepts of history and identify and explain historical relationships.

Learning Expectations

TCC.1.1	Examine and analyze stories of important Americans and their contributions to our society.
TCC.1.2	Explain how individuals, events and ideas influence the history of one's self, family, community, state and nation.
TCC.1.5	Recognize the historical significance of national holidays and symbols.

Activity

Title: | **Lesson 14 - Button String**

Sources:

1) *Activities for Elementary School Social Studies*, pages 3.10-3.11 Adaptation

Materials Needed:

1) lots of buttons in many colors and shapes
2) heavy thread or yarn
3) embroidery needle optional

Objectives:

As a result of this activity, the student will:
o understand the practice of keeping unused buttons
o select many colors and shapes of buttons for making a button string
o produce a button string as beautiful as possible

Introduction:

1) Show a model of a button string.
2) Explain collecting unused buttons from wherever possible, because buttons were too precious to throw away.
3) Pass out a variety of colors and shapes of buttons to look at.

Major Instructional Sequence:

4) Collect and assemble materials they will need.
5) Working alone or in cooperative groups, have students design a button string.
6) Construct button string with contrasting colors and shapes.

Concluding Sequence/Closure:

7) Let students share about their button string with the class.
8) Display the button strings as an exhibit.

Performance Assessment Task

Title:	**Lesson 14 - Button String**

Name:		Grade:	K-4
Date:		Subject:	Social Studies

Alignment to State Standards:
(minimum of three standards, input State standards below)

Code	Standard Description

Description of Performance Task:
(include time, student performance, assessment)

Time:	30 minutes (approx.)
Activity:	Activity will correlate with reading *On the Banks of Plum Creek*.
Task:	o Student will select several colors and shapes of buttons.
	o Student will explain about the practice of keeping unused button.
	o Student will collect and examine many colors and shapes of buttons.
	o Student will produce a button string using different colors and shapes of buttons.
	o Student will share about the button string with the class.
	o Student will display the button string.

Student Scoring Guide: (attach a copy)

Teacher Scoring Guide: (attach a copy of scoring key)

Score (select one): [4] Exemplary [3] Proficient [2] Apprentice [1] Novice

Student Scoring Guide

Title: **Lesson 14 - Button String**

Name:

😊☹ I selected several colors and shapes of buttons.

😊☹ I explained about the practice of keeping unused buttons.

😊☹ I examined lots of beautiful colors and shapes of buttons.

😊☹ I produced a beautiful button string using lots of colors and shapes.

😊☹ I displayed my button string in an exhibit.

Little House Social Studies Curriculum Guide ©2005

Teacher Scoring Guide

Title: **Lesson 14 - Button String**

[4] Exemplary	o Effectively compiles several colors and shapes of buttons.
	o Clearly addresses and interprets the practice of keeping unused buttons.
	o Handles well producing a beautiful button string using different colors and shapes.
	o Few errors displaying exhibit of button string.

[3] Proficient	o Appropriately differentiates several colors and shapes of buttons.
	o Fairly strong relating to the practice of keeping unused buttons.
	o Some errors producing a beautiful button string using different colors and shapes.
	o Some errors displaying exhibit of button string.

[2] Apprentice	o Not elaborate selection of several colors and shapes of buttons.
	o Significant weakness explaining about the practice of keeping unused buttons.
	o Not focusing on producing a beautiful button string using different colors and shapes.
	o Many errors displaying exhibit of button string.

[1] Novice	o Little or no naming of several colors and shapes of buttons.
	o Very little identification of the practice of keeping unused buttons.
	o Lacks producing a beautiful button string using different colors and shapes.
	o Serious errors displaying exhibit of button string.

Lesson Plan

Title:	**Lesson 15 - Christmas Popcorn Ball**

Date:		Grade:	K-4

Suggested Season / Date: Winter / December, week 3

Time: 30 minutes (approx.)

Subject: Social Studies, Anthropology Activities

Learning Style / Different Multiple Intelligences: Tactile/Kinesthetic; Naturalistic Intelligences (activity could be used for all areas)

Example: hands on, doing, touching, study natural phenomenon and learn how things work, popping corn and making popcorn ball

Materials Needed:

1) *On the Banks of Plum Creek*, pages 171-255
2) *The Little House Cookbook*, pages 216-217
3) *The World of Little House*, pages 51-53
4) *Activities for Elementary School Social Studies*, pages 3.6-3.7 Adaptation
5) *Little House Social Studies Curriculum Guide*, Activity, Performance Assessment Task, Student Scoring Guide, Teacher Scoring Guide: Lesson 15 - Christmas Popcorn Ball

Introduction:

1) Read from *On the Banks of Plum Creek*.
2) Discuss uses for popcorn at Christmas: stringing popcorn, popcorn balls for eating and making popcorn ball ornaments.
3) The purpose is to learn about how to make popcorn balls and use popcorn at Christmas.

Major Instructional Sequence:

4) Provide information about ways Laura and her family used popcorn at Christmas.
5) Modeling: Provide examples of popcorn balls, popcorn ball ornament and popcorn on a string for hanging on the Christmas tree.
6) Ask questions for understanding about uses of popcorn.

Concluding Sequence/Closure:

7) *Little House Social Studies Curriculum Guide*, Activity: Lesson 15 - Christmas Popcorn Ball

Evaluation:

8) *Little House Social Studies Curriculum Guide*, Performance Assessment Task, Student Scoring Guide, Teacher Scoring Guide: Lesson 15 - Christmas Popcorn Ball

Alignment to State Standards:

(compare to standards shown: Arkansas)

Strand 2:	People, Places and Environments
Content Standard 1:	Students will demonstrate an understanding that people, cultures and systems are connected and that commonalities and diversities exist among them.

Learning Expectations

PPE.1.2	Compare and contrast similarities and differences in cultures through a variety of experiences, such as reading, writing, drawing, role-playing, dance, music and simulation.
PPE.1.3	Analyze the contributions of various groups to community, state and nation.
PPE.1.6	Distinguish similarities and differences among families and communities around the world.

Activity

Title: | **Lesson 15 - Christmas Popcorn Ball**

Sources:

1) *Activities for Elementary School Social Studies*, pages 3.6-3.7 Adaptation

Materials Needed:

1) popped corn, six quarts
2) molasses, two cups
3) butter, four tablespoons
4) baking sheets

Objectives:

As a result of this activity, the student will:
o produce a popcorn ball
o realize that people used popcorn for stringing popcorn and making popcorn ball ornaments for Christmas

Introduction:

1) Show a model of a popcorn ball, popcorn ball ornament and popcorn strands done previously.
2) Tell students that people used to frequently made popcorn balls.
3) Relate how people used popcorn for Christmas.
4) Tell students that they will make their own popcorn ball.

Major Instructional Sequence:

5) Have students spread butter on the baking sheets.
6) Have student butter their hands for holding popcorn.
7) Demonstrate how to form the molasses and popcorn into a ball.
8) Spread the molasses (teacher will prepare the molasses) over the popcorn quickly and shape into popcorn balls.
9) Place popcorn balls on baking sheets to cool.

Concluding Sequence/Closure:

10) Have students show and tell about their popcorn balls.
11) Display the popcorn balls. Store in bags for taking home/or eat at school.

Little House Social Studies Curriculum Guide ©2005

Performance Assessment Task

Title:	**Lesson 15 - Christmas Popcorn Ball**

Name:		Grade:	K-4
Date:		Subject:	Social Studies

Alignment to State Standards:
(minimum of three standards, input State standards below)

Code	Standard Description

Description of Performance Task:
(include time, student performance, assessment)

Time:	30 minutes (approx.)
Activity:	Activity will correlate with reading *On the Banks of Plum Creek*.
Task:	o Student will recall and relate how Laura and her family made popcorn for stringing popcorn, popcorn ornaments and eating popcorn balls. o Student will demonstrate producing a popcorn ball. o Student will show and tell about their popcorn ball. o Student will display in bag for storage. o Student may eat popcorn ball when activity is finished (or take home).

Student Scoring Guide: (attach a copy)

Teacher Scoring Guide: (attach a copy of scoring key)

Score (select one): [4] Exemplary [3] Proficient [2] Apprentice [1] Novice

Student Scoring Guide

Title: 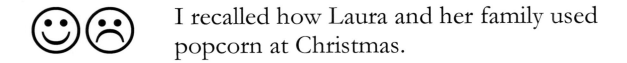 **Lesson 15 - Christmas Popcorn Ball**

Name:

☺ ☹ I recalled how Laura and her family used popcorn at Christmas.

☺ ☹ I discussed popcorn balls, stringing popcorn and popcorn ornaments.

☺ ☹ I produced a popcorn ball.

☺ ☹ I told about my popcorn ball.

☺ ☹ I displayed my popcorn ball.

Teacher Scoring Guide

Title: **Lesson 15 - Christmas Popcorn Ball**

[4] Exemplary
- o Effective summary of how Laura and her family used popcorn at Christmas.
- o Clearly contrasts how popcorn is used for stringing, ornaments and popcorn balls.
- o Few errors creating a popcorn ball.
- o Fluently summarizes about a popcorn ball.

[3] Proficient
- o Reasonably applies how Laura and her family used popcorn at Christmas.
- o Appropriately differentiates how popcorn is used for stringing, ornaments and popcorn balls.
- o Some errors producing a popcorn ball.
- o Ideas progress relating to a popcorn ball.

[2] Apprentice
- o Not much information explaining how Laura and her family used popcorn at Christmas.
- o Repetitive summary of how popcorn is used for stringing, ornaments and popcorn balls.
- o Many errors producing a popcorn ball.
- o Not focusing on describing a popcorn ball.

[1] Novice
- o Unclear naming how Laura and her family used popcorn at Christmas.
- o Little or no stating of how popcorn is used for stringing, ornaments and popcorn balls.
- o Little or no production of a popcorn ball.
- o Serious errors describing a popcorn ball.

Lesson Plan

Title:	**Lesson 16 - Thimble Pictures**

		Grade:	K-4
Date:			

Suggested Season / Date: Winter / December, week 4

Time: 30 minutes (approx.)

Subject: Social Studies, History Activities

Learning Style / Different Multiple Intelligences: Tactile/Kinesthetic; Bodily/Kinesthetic Intelligences (activity could be used for all areas)

Example: hands on, moving and touching, interact with space around them, handling objects, pressing thimbles in to frost on windows (options).

Materials Needed:

1) *On the Banks of Plum Creek*, pages 256-339
2) *The World of Little House*, page 59
3) *Across the Curriculum with Favorite Authors*, page 56
4) *Activities for Elementary School Social Studies*, page 2.22 Adaptation
5) *Little House Social Studies Curriculum Guide*, Activity, Performance Assessment Task, Student Scoring Guide, Teacher Scoring Guide: Lesson 16 - Thimble Pictures

Introduction:

1) Read from *On the Banks of Plum Creek*.
2) Use a variety of sources to show different ways to achieve thimble pictures in the frost on a windowpane.
3) The purpose is to learn to make pictures using thimbles.

Major Instructional Sequence:

4) Show and discuss various ways to make thimble pictures.
5) Model making a thimble picture.
6) Check for understanding.

Concluding Sequence/Closure:

7) *Little House Social Studies Curriculum Guide*, Activity: Lesson 16 - Thimble Pictures

Evaluation:

8) *Little House Social Studies Curriculum Guide*, Performance Assessment Task, Student Scoring Guide, Teacher Scoring Guide: Lesson 16 - Thimble Pictures

Alignment to State Standards:

(compare to standards shown: Arkansas)

Strand 1:	Time, Continuity and Change
Content Standard 2:	Students will demonstrate an understanding of how ideas, events and conditions bring about change.

Learning Expectations

TCC.2.3	Use personal experiences, biographies, autobiographies or historical fiction to explain how individuals are affected by, can cope with and can create change.
TCC.2.4	Explain how people, places, events, tools, institutions, attitudes, values and ideas are the result of what has gone before.
TCC.2.5	Use a variety of processes, such as thinking, reading, writing, listening and speaking, to demonstrate continuity and change.

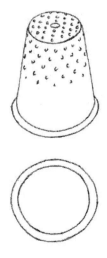
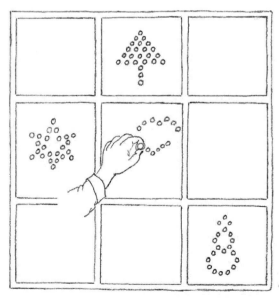

Activity

Title: **Lesson 16 - Thimble Pictures**

Sources:

1) *Activities for Elementary School Social Studies*, page 2.22 Adaptation

Materials Needed:

1) thimbles or bottle caps
2) frosty windowpane (hopefully)
3) ink pad and paper (optional)
4) shallow pan and sugar, cornmeal or sand (optional)
5) pencils and paper (optional)

Objectives:

As a result of this activity, the student will:
o create thimble pictures using their own thimble and tools
o select various pictures to design on the windowpane
o produce a thimble pictures in various panes if possible
o optional to design thimble pictures using other mediums

Introduction:

1) Model creating a thimble picture, using frosty windowpane.
2) Explain how Laura and family used to draw pictures using thimbles.
3) Discuss various thimble pictures Laura and her family might have drawn, as a Christmas tree, birds flying, log house with smoke coming out of the chimney or even a roly-poly man and a roly-poly woman.

Major Instructional Sequence:

4) Pass out thimbles for using on frost or, if necessary, another mode.
5) Press the thimble in to the frost and make a design.
6) Construct a variety of pictures by pressing the thimble in to the frost.

Concluding Sequence/Closure:

7) Let students share about their thimble pictures in the frost.
8) View the thimble pictures while the frost is still on the windowpanes.

Little House Social Studies Curriculum Guide ©2005

Performance Assessment Task

Title:	**Lesson 16 - Thimble Pictures**		

Name:		Grade:	K-4
Date:		Subject:	Social Studies

Alignment to State Standards:
(minimum of three standards, input State standards below)

Code	Standard Description

Description of Performance Task:
(include time, student performance, assessment)

Time:	30 minutes (approx.)
Activity:	Activity will correlate with reading *On the Banks of Plum Creek*.
Task:	o Student will list various thimble pictures: Christmas tree, birds flying, a roly-poly man and roly-poly woman. o Student will explain how Laura's family drew pictures using thimbles. o Student will press thimble in to the frost on the windowpane frost. o If frost is not available, another mode can be used: ink pad and paper; shallow pan of sugar, cornmeal or sand; bottle cap, pencils and paper. o Student will imagine the kinds of pictures Laura might have drawn. o Student will exhibit their thimble pictures and view while the frost is on the windowpane.

Student Scoring Guide:	(attach a copy)

Teacher Scoring Guide:	(attach a copy of scoring key)
Score (select one):	[4] Exemplary [3] Proficient [2] Apprentice [1] Novice

Student Scoring Guide

Title: **Lesson 16 - Thimble Pictures**

Name:

😊😦 I listed various thimble pictures: Christmas tree, birds flying, a roly-poly man and a roly-poly woman.

😊😦 I explained how Laura and her family used to draw pictures using thimbles.

😊😦 I used a variety of mediums to demonstrate thimble pictures.

😊😦 I imagined the kinds of pictures Laura might have drawn using thimbles.

😊😦 I exhibited my thimble picture on the window frost until it melted (if applicable).

Little House Social Studies Curriculum Guide ©2005

Teacher Scoring Guide

Title: | **Lesson 16 - Thimble Pictures**

---

[4] Exemplary
- o Effectively supports possible thimble pictures.
- o Clearly addresses various mediums to produce thimble pictures.
- o Fluently imagines and shares kinds of thimble pictures Laura might have drawn.
- o Handles well exhibiting thimble pictures.

---

[3] Proficient
- o Reasonably differentiates possible thimble pictures.
- o May have some weakness demonstrating various mediums to produce thimble pictures.
- o Appropriately imagines kinds of thimble pictures that Laura might have drawn.
- o Reasonably portrays thimble pictures.

---

[2] Apprentice
- o Not elaborate predicting of possible thimble pictures.
- o Inconsistent converting various mediums to produce thimble pictures.
- o Not able to focus on kinds of thimble pictures that Laura might have drawn.
- o Significant weakness in portraying thimble pictures.

---

[1] Novice
- o Little or no listing of possible thimble pictures.
- o Unclear use of various mediums to produce thimble pictures.
- o Lacks imagination for kinds of thimble pictures that Laura might have drawn.
- o Unclear exhibition of thimble pictures.

Lesson Plan

Title:	**Lesson 17 - Model Trains**

Date:		Grade:	K-4

Suggested Season / Date: | Winter / January, week 1

Time: | 30 minutes (approx.)

Subject: | Social Studies, Geography Activities

Learning Style / Different Multiple Intelligences: | Tactile/Kinesthetic; Visual/Spatial Intelligences (activity could be used for all areas)

Example: | exploring physical objects, perceive the visual in pictures, videos and maps of trains

Materials Needed:

1) *By the Shores of Silver Lake*, pages 1-73
2) *Little House in the Classroom*, page 73
3) *Across the Curriculum with Favorite Authors*, page 64
4) *The World of Little House*, pages 63-64, 67-68
5) *Activities for Elementary School Social Studies*, pages 1.4-1.5 Adaptation
6) *Little House Social Studies Curriculum Guide*, Activity, Performance Assessment Task, Student Scoring Guide, Teacher Scoring Guide: Lesson 17 - Model Trains

Introduction:

1) Read from *By the Shores of Silver Lake*.
2) Show videos, pictures, computer slide shows and models of trains.
3) The purpose is to compare the differences between model and real trains.

Little House Social Studies Curriculum Guide ©2005

Major Instructional Sequence:

4) View video, pictures, model trains and examine them.
5) Distinguish between representations of model trains and the real thing.
6) Ask questions for understanding.

Concluding Sequence/Closure:

7) *Little House Social Studies Curriculum Guide*, Activity: Lesson 17 - Model Trains

Evaluation:

8) *Little House Social Studies Curriculum Guide*, Performance Assessment Task, Student Scoring Guide, Teacher Scoring Guide: Lesson 17 - Model Trains

Alignment to State Standards:

(compare to standards shown: Arkansas)

Strand 2:	People, Places and Environments
Content Standard 2:	Students will demonstrate an understanding of the significance of physical and cultural characteristics of places and world regions.

Learning Expectations

PPE.2.1	Explain how geography and the environment affect the way people live.
PPE.2.4	Understand the various types of maps and their uses.
PPE.2.6	Explore and communicate how technology affects geography.

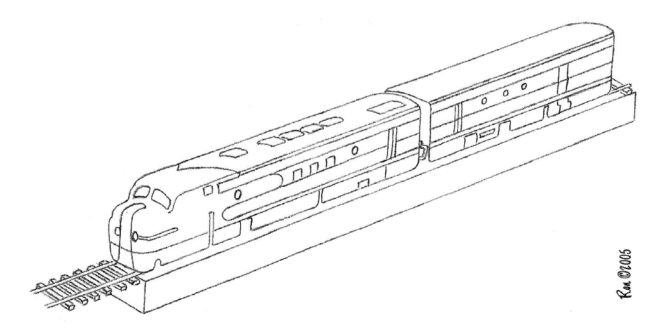

Rm.©2005

Activity

Title: | **Lesson 17 - Model Trains**

Sources:

1) *Activities for Elementary School Social Studies*, pages 1.4-1.5 Adaptation

Materials Needed:

1) models of train cars
2) pictures, videos, computer examples (such as screensavers)
3) map of train tracks and train station

Objectives:

As a result of this activity, the student will:
o distinguish between train models and the real thing
o distinguish between pictures, videos and the real thing
o distinguish between mapped representations and the real thing

Introduction:

1) Place the models, pictures and picture maps on a table and invite the students to explore the objects on the table.
2) Have students hold the model trains and examine them closely.
3) Let students view brief video and computer screensavers of trains.

Major Instructional Sequence:

4) Have students gather around the table in a large, loose circle.
5) Hold up models and ask questions. Elaborate on the fact that it is a model of a real train, pictures and map representation.
6) Call attention to a brief video of trains and screensavers on computer.

Concluding Sequence/Closure:

7) Have each student select an object from the table.
8) Take turns letting each student explain what he/she is holding and how it relates to the real thing. Continue until each student has had a turn to compare a model, picture or map to a representation.
9) Let students talk about what they saw in the video and on the computer and how that relates to the real thing.

Little House Social Studies Curriculum Guide ©2005

Performance Assessment Task

Title: **Lesson 17 - Model Trains**

Name:

Date:

Grade: K-4

Subject: Social Studies

Alignment to State Standards:
(minimum of three standards, input State standards below)

Code	Standard Description

Description of Performance Task:
(include time, student performance, assessment)

Time: 30 minutes (approx.)

Activity: Activity will correlate with reading *By the Shores of Silver Lake*.

Task:
- o Student will view model trains, pictures, maps, videos and computer screensavers of trains.
- o Student will explain about the representation and real trains.
- o Student will examine and explore representations of the real train.
- o Student will differentiate between model and the real trains.
- o Student will compare and contrast between model and real trains.

Student Scoring Guide: (attach a copy)

Teacher Scoring Guide: (attach a copy of scoring key)

Score (select one): [4] Exemplary [3] Proficient [2] Apprentice [1] Novice

Student Scoring Guide

Title: **Lesson 17 - Model Trains**

Name:

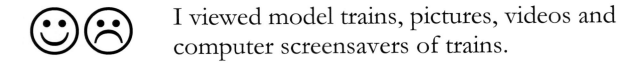 I viewed model trains, pictures, videos and computer screensavers of trains.

😊😞 I explained about the representation of a model train and a real train.

😊😞 I examined and explored representations of real trains.

😊😞 I differentiated between model and real trains.

😊😞 I compared and contrasted between model and real trains.

Teacher Scoring Guide

Title: **Lesson 17 - Model Trains**

[4] Exemplary	o Effectively views model trains, pictures, videos and computer screensavers of trains.
	o Clearly examines and explores the differences between representations and real trains.
	o Fluently interprets differences between model and real trains.
	o Consistently compares and contrasts between model and real trains.

[3] Proficient	o Focuses on viewing model trains, pictures, videos and computer screensavers of trains.
	o Reasonably distinguishes the differences between representations and real trains.
	o Appropriately deduces differences between model and real trains.
	o Fairly strongly differentiates between model and real trains.

[2] Apprentice	o Not focusing on viewing model trains, pictures, videos and computer screensavers of trains.
	o Inconsistency in distinguishing the differences between representations and real trains.
	o Weak progression discussing differences between model and the real trains.
	o No particular order generalizing between model and real trains.

[1] Novice	o Little or no viewing of model trains, pictures and computer screensavers of trains.
	o Lacks naming the differences between representations and real trains.
	o Does not recall differences between model and real trains.
	o Incomplete selecting between model and real trains.

Lesson Plan

Title:	**Lesson 18 - Railroad Past & Present**

Date:		Grade:	K-4

Suggested Season / Date:	Winter / January, week 2

Time:	30 minutes (approx.)

Subject:	Social Studies, History Activities

Learning Style / Different Multiple Intelligences:	Visual; Interpersonal Intelligence (activity could be used for all areas)

Example:	seeing visuals, magazines, pictures, newspapers, catalogs, organize and cooperate as a group

Materials Needed:

1) *By the Shores of Silver Lake*, pages 74-146
2) *Little House in the Classroom*, pages 73, 77
3) *The World of Little House*, pages 67-70
4) *Across the Curriculum with Favorite Authors*, pages 64-65
5) *Activities for Elementary School Social Studies*, pages 2.6-2.7 Adaptation
6) *Little House Social Studies Curriculum Guide*, Activity, Performance Assessment Task, Student Scoring Guide, Teacher Scoring Guide: Lesson 18 - Railroad Past & Present

Introduction:

1) Read from *By the Shores of Silver Lake*.
2) Show pictures of trains, past and present, discuss and share information about Laura watching the railroad being built.
3) The purpose is to learn about the railroad, past and present.

Major Instructional Sequence:

4) Show pictures and models of trains and examine them. Discuss differences between trains, then and now. Explain concepts concerning the Ingalls life during the building of the railroad.
5) Model, allowing time for questions about trains, then and now.
6) Check for understanding.

Concluding Sequence/Closure:

7) *Little House Social Studies Curriculum Guide*, Activity: Lesson 18 - Railroad Past & Present

Evaluation:

8) *Little House Social Studies Curriculum Guide*, Performance Assessment Task, Student Scoring Guide, Teacher Scoring Guide: Lesson 18 - Railroad Past & Present

Alignment to State Standards:

(compare to standards shown: Arkansas)

Strand 1:	Time, Continuity and Change
Content Standard 1:	Students will demonstrate an understanding of the chronology and concepts of history and identify and explain historical relationships.

Learning Expectations

TCC.1.1	Examine and analyze stories of important Americans and their contributions to our society.
TCC.1.3	Demonstrate the ability to think in terms of sequencing events.
TCC.1.4	Describe how history is a continuing story of events, people and places.

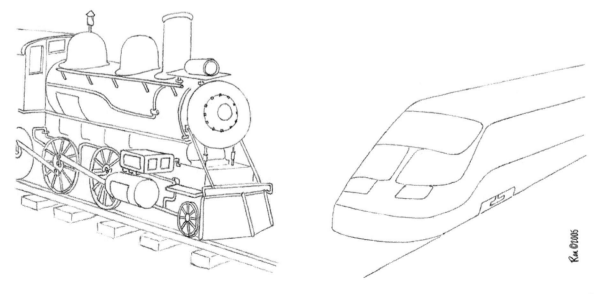

Activity

Title: **Lesson 18 - Railroad Past & Present**

Sources:

1) *Activities for Elementary School Social Studies*, pages 2.6-2.7 Adaptation

Materials Needed:

1) old magazines, newspapers, catalogs, archival pictures of trains from long ago to present
2) poster board
3) marking pens
4) scissors, glue

Objectives:

As a result of this activity, the student will:
o interpret and display information in graphic form
o create a chart to display trains to move people now and long ago
o work cooperatively in groups

Introduction:

1) Place the models, pictures and picture maps on a table and invite the students to explore the objects on the table.
2) Have students hold the model trains and examine them closely.
3) Let students view brief video and computer screensavers of trains.

Major Instructional Sequence:

4) Divide students into cooperative work groups.
5) Groups work together to search for pictures of trains, then and now.
6) Students cut out pictures and glue them on poster board according to timeline.
7) Circulate among groups, checking for understanding.

Concluding Sequence/Closure:

8) Groups show and tell about their posters, identifying the trains, then and now. (Make sure all students in the group have opportunity to participate in the group's presentation.)
9) Posters are hung for display on the bulletin board.

Little House Social Studies Curriculum Guide ©2005

Performance Assessment Task

Title:	**Lesson 18 - Railroad Past & Present**		

Name:		Grade:	K-4
Date:		Subject:	Social Studies

Alignment to State Standards:
(minimum of three standards, input State standards below)

Code	Standard Description

Description of Performance Task:
(include time, student performance, assessment)

Time:	30 minutes (approx.)
Activity:	Activity will correlate with reading *By the Shores of Silver Lake*.
Task:	<ul><li>Student will identify trains, then and now, according to timeline.</li><li>Student will understand the concept of "then to now," according to timeline.</li><li>Student will cooperate to search for pictures of trains, then to now.</li><li>Student will cut out pictures and glue them on the poster board according to timeline.</li><li>Student will differentiate between trains, then and now, according to timeline.</li><li>Student will (groups) will display train poster on the bulletin board.</li></ul>

Student Scoring Guide:	(attach a copy)

Teacher Scoring Guide:	(attach a copy of scoring key)
Score (select one):	[4] Exemplary [3] Proficient [2] Apprentice [1] Novice

Student Scoring Guide

Title: | **Lesson 18 - Railroad Past & Present**

Name:

☺☹   I identified trains, then and now, according to a timeline.

☺☹   I understood the timeline, then to now.

☺☹   I used pictures to cut and glue on poster board, according to the timeline, then to now.

☺☹   I differentiated between trains, then and now, according to timeline.

☺☹   I displayed the train timeline poster on the bulletin board.

Teacher Scoring Guide

Title: | **Lesson 18 - Railroad Past & Present**

---

[4] Exemplary
- o Fluently interprets trains, then to now, according to timeline.
- o Effectively compiles pictures of trains, then to now, according to timeline.
- o Consistently categorizes train pictures on poster board.
- o Handles well displaying train poster on bulletin board.

---

[3] Proficient
- o Clearly outlines trains, then to now, according to timeline.
- o Reasonably understands pictures of trains, then to now, according to timeline.
- o Appropriately differentiates train pictures on poster board.
- o Fairly strong demonstration of train poster on bulletin board.

---

[2] Apprentice
- o Inconsistent explaining trains, then to now, according to timeline.
- o Not too clear outlining of pictures of trains, then to now, according to timeline.
- o No particular order of train pictures on poster board.
- o Not much information on train poster, then to now, on bulletin board.

---

[1] Novice
- o Lacks evidence of naming trains, then to now, according to timeline.
- o Not able to recall pictures of trains, then to now, according to timeline.
- o Repeated errors listing train pictures on poster board.
- o Little or no display of train poster, then to now, on bulletin board.

Lesson Plan

Title:	**Lesson 19 - Checkers**

Date:		Grade:	K-4

Suggested Season / Date: | Winter / January, week 3

Time: | 30 minutes (approx.)

Subject: | Social Studies, History Activities

Learning Style / Different Multiple Intelligences: | Tactile/Kinesthetic; Logical/Mathematical Intelligences (activity could be used for all areas)

Example: | hands on, moving and touching, ability to use reason, logic and numbers and work with checkers

Materials Needed:

1) *By the Shores of Silver Lake*, pages 147-219
2) *Little House in the Classroom*, page 79
3) *Across the Curriculum with Favorite Authors*, pages 66, 73
4) *Activities for Elementary School Social Studies*, page 2.13 Adaptation
5) *Little House Social Studies Curriculum Guide*, Activity, Performance Assessment Task, Student Scoring Guide, Teacher Scoring Guide: Lesson 19 - Checkers

Introduction:

1) Read from *By the Shores of Silver Lake*.
2) Discuss checkers and Chinese checkers.
3) The purpose is to learn to play checkers and Chinese checkers.

Major Instructional Sequence:

4) Instruct students on how to play and the rules for checkers and Chinese checkers. Talk about how Pa made the game for Laura.
5) Model playing checkers and Chinese checkers.
6) Ask questions for understanding.

Concluding Sequence/Closure:

7) *Little House Social Studies Curriculum Guide*, Activity: Lesson 19 - Checkers

Evaluation:

8) *Little House Social Studies Curriculum Guide*, Performance Assessment Task, Student Scoring Guide, Teacher Scoring Guide: Lesson 19 - Checkers

Alignment to State Standards:

(compare to standards shown: Arkansas)

Strand 1:	Time, Continuity and Change
Content Standard 2:	Students will demonstrate an understanding of how ideas, events and conditions bring about change.

Learning Expectations

TCC.2.3	Use personal experiences, biographies, autobiographies or historical fiction to explain how individuals are affected by, can cope with and can create change.
TCC.2.4	Explain how people, places, events, tools, institutions, attitudes, values and ideas are the result of what has gone before.
TCC.2.5	Use a variety of processes, such as thinking, reading, writing, listening and speaking, to demonstrate continuity and change.

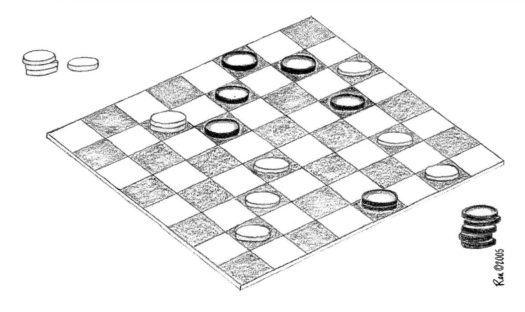

Activity

Title: | **Lesson 19 - Checkers**

Sources:

1) *Activities for Elementary School Social Studies*, page 2.13 Adaptation

Materials Needed:

1) checker boards
2) checkers
3) Chinese checker boards
4) marbles

Objectives:

As a result of this activity, the student will:
o interact with other students in a cooperative learning environment
o match information learned when broken up into pairs
o learn to play checkers
o learn to play Chinese checkers

Introduction:

1) Tell students they will pair off to play checkers or Chinese checkers.
2) Show students how the games are set up.

Major Instructional Sequence:

3) Divide students into cooperative work groups (four or five groups).
4) Give each group a game set up to play.
5) Have each student take a turn learning to play either game.
6) After one game is played, students may trade games.

Concluding Sequence/Closure:

7) Let students tell about their games: the easiest and the most difficult.
8) Have students show that they remember how to play checkers or Chinese checkers.

Little House Social Studies Curriculum Guide ©2005

Performance Assessment Task

Title: | **Lesson 19 - Checkers**

Name: | Grade: | K-4

Date: | Subject: | Social Studies

Alignment to State Standards:
(minimum of three standards, input State standards below)

Code	Standard Description

Description of Performance Task:
(include time, student performance, assessment)

Time: | 30 minutes (approx.)

Activity: | Activity will correlate with reading *By the Shores of Silver Lake*.

Task:
- o Student will state what checkers and Chinese checkers are.
- o Student will explain how to play checkers and Chinese checkers.
- o Student will use a variety of ways to play checkers and Chinese checkers.
- o Student will formulate different ways to play checkers and Chinese checkers.
- o Student will perform checkers and Chinese checkers with other players.

Student Scoring Guide: | (attach a copy)

Teacher Scoring Guide: | (attach a copy of scoring key)

Score (select one): | [4] Exemplary [3] Proficient [2] Apprentice [1] Novice

Student Scoring Guide

Title: | **Lesson 19 - Checkers**

Name:

 I stated what checkers and Chinese checkers are.

 I explained how to play checkers and Chinese checkers.

 I used a variety of ways to play checkers and Chinese checkers.

 I formulated different ways to play checkers and Chinese checkers.

 I performed checkers and Chinese checkers playing with other players.

Teacher Scoring Guide

Title:	Lesson 19 - Checkers

[4] Exemplary	o Effectively interprets how to play checkers and Chinese checkers. o Imaginative in identifying a variety of ways to play checkers and Chinese checkers. o Consistently formulates different ways to play checkers and Chinese checkers. o Contains few errors performing checkers and Chinese checkers playing with others.
[3] Proficient	o Appropriately outlines how to play checkers and Chinese checkers. o Fairly strong in identifying a variety of ways to play checkers and Chinese checkers. o Some errors modifying different ways to play checkers and Chinese checkers. o Focuses on performing checkers and Chinese checkers playing with others.
[2] Apprentice	o Not too clear in explaining how to play checkers and Chinese checkers. o Not focusing on identifying a variety of ways to play checkers and Chinese checkers. o Inconsistent estimating different ways to play checkers and Chinese checkers. o Many errors performing checkers and Chinese checkers playing with others.
[1] Novice	o Lacks evidence of stating how to play checkers and Chinese checkers. o Difficulty in identifying a variety of ways to play checkers and Chinese checkers. o Repeated errors defining different ways to play checkers and Chinese checkers. o Little or no performing checkers and Chinese checkers playing with others.

Lesson Plan

Title:	**Lesson 20 - Moving Day**
Date:	Grade: K-4
Suggested Season / Date:	Winter / January, week 4
Time:	30 minutes (approx.)
Subject:	Social Studies, Geography Activities
Learning Style / Different Multiple Intelligences:	Tactile/Kinesthetic; Visual/Spatial Intelligences (activity could be used for all areas)
Example:	hands on, doing and touching, design a map of travel

Materials Needed:

1) *By the Shores of Silver Lake*, pages 220-290
2) *Across the Curriculum with Favorite Authors*, pages 68, 75
3) *The World of Little House*, pages 64-66
4) *Activities for Elementary School Social Studies*, pages 1.6-1.7 Adaptation
5) *Little House Social Studies Curriculum Guide*, Activity, Performance Assessment Task, Student Scoring Guide, Teacher Scoring Guide: Lesson 20 - Moving Day

Introduction:

1) Read from *By the Shores of Silver Lake*.
2) Share information about Laura moving from the Surveyor's house in town to the claim shanty/homestead in the country.
3) The purpose is to learn about what it is like to move.

Major Instructional Sequence:

4) Provide information about Laura's family's moving process. Describe both locations: Surveyor's house and homestead in the country. Also, discuss needs along the way.

5) Show maps and pictures of the move.

6) Ask questions for understanding about the moving process.

Concluding Sequence/Closure:

7) *Little House Social Studies Curriculum Guide*, Activity: Lesson 20 - Moving Day

Evaluation:

8) *Little House Social Studies Curriculum Guide*, Performance Assessment Task, Student Scoring Guide, Teacher Scoring Guide: Lesson 20 - Moving Day

Alignment to State Standards:

(compare to standards shown: Arkansas)

Strand 2:	People, Places and Environments
Content Standard 2:	Students will demonstrate an understanding of the significance of physical and cultural characteristics of places and world regions.

Learning Expectations

PPE.2.1	Explain how geography and the environment affect the way people live.
PPE.2.2	Understand and apply the five themes of geography: location, place, human-environment interaction, movement and regions.
PPE.2.3	Compare and contrast the features of rural and urban areas.

Activity

Title: **Lesson 20 - Moving Day**

Sources:

1) *Activities for Elementary School Social Studies*, pages 1.6-1.7 Adaptation

Materials Needed:

1) long strips of butcher paper (15-20 feet long)
2) empty milk cartons, cereal boxes (to represent buildings)
3) toy horses and buggy
4) marking pens

Objectives:

As a result of this activity, the student will:
o construct the travel that Laura and her family made
o think of needs people might encounter along the way; how their travels would be
o create what surveyor house and claim shanty looked like at both ends

Introduction:

1) Move the furniture from the center of the classroom and stretch the paper out.
2) Have students sit along each side of the paper strip. Tell them the strip is where they moved from the surveyor's house to the claim shanty.
3) Drive the toy horse and buggy along the pathway and tell about how the long the trip would have taken them from the surveyor's house to the homestead.

Major Instructional Sequence:

4) Ask the students to draw the surveyor's house at one end; ask what it looked like.
5) Go to the center to draw what it might have looked like traveling along the way.
6) Help place cartons for buildings where there might have been in the town.
7) Discuss what the claim shanty area looked like in the country and lead other students to draw that area with markers.

Concluding Sequence/Closure:

8) Work in cooperative groups to draw the map on butcher paper, using milk cartons and marking pens.
9) Hang the map as exhibit in the classroom.

Little House Social Studies Curriculum Guide ©2005

Performance Assessment Task

Title: **Lesson 20 - Moving Day**

Name:

Date:

Grade: K-4

Subject: Social Studies

Alignment to State Standards:
(minimum of three standards, input State standards below)

Code	Standard Description

Description of Performance Task:
(include time, student performance, assessment)

Time: 30 minutes (approx.)

Activity: Activity will correlate with reading *By the Shores of Silver Lake*.

Task:
- o Student will chart the route Laura's family took from the homestead in the country to the Surveyor's house.
- o Student will explain and understand the locations.
- o Student will (group) will work cooperatively to create the travel from the homestead in the country to the Surveyor's house.
- o Student will use milk cartons/markers to display homes and travel.
- o Student will differentiate between the locations.
- o Student will compare and contrast the move from the homestead in the country to the Surveyor's house.

Student Scoring Guide: (attach a copy)

Teacher Scoring Guide: (attach a copy of scoring key)

Score (select one): [4] Exemplary [3] Proficient [2] Apprentice [1] Novice

Student Scoring Guide

Title: **Lesson 20 - Moving Day**

Name:

 I charted the route Laura's family made from the homestead in the country to the Surveyor's house.

 I explained and understood the location of the homestead in the country and the Surveyor's house.

 I demonstrated by depicting the move on my section of the butcher paper.

 I differentiated between the location of the homestead in the country and the Surveyor's house.

 I compared and contrasted the move between the homestead in the country and the Surveyor's house.

Little House Social Studies Curriculum Guide ©2005

Teacher Scoring Guide

Title: | **Lesson 20 - Moving Day**

---

[4] Exemplary

o Effectively charts the route Laura's family took from the homestead in the country to the Surveyor's house.
o Controlled use of marking pens and milk cartons to demonstrate the moving process.
o Handles well supporting a contribution for the move on butcher paper.
o Compares and contrasts the move from the homestead in the country to the Surveyor's house.

---

[3] Proficient

o Appropriately explains the route Laura's family took from the homestead in the country to the Surveyor's house.
o Some weakness using marking pens and milk cartons to demonstrate the moving process.
o Reasonable depiction of a contribution for the move on butcher paper.
o Some errors in relating the move from the homestead in the country to the Surveyor's house.

---

[2] Apprentice

o Not clear discriminating the route Laura's family took from the homestead in the country to the Surveyor's house.
o Not elaborate use of marking pens and milk cartons to demonstrate the moving process.
o Inconsistent predicting of a contribution for the move on butcher paper.
o Repetitive paraphrasing the move from the homestead in the country to the Surveyor's house.

---

[1] Novice

o Little or no identifying of the route Laura's family took from the homestead in the country to the Surveyors' house.
o Lacks in use of marking pens and milk cartons to demonstrate the moving process.
o Very little labeling of a contribution for the move on butcher paper.
o Serious errors stating the move from the homestead in the country to the Surveyor's house.

Lesson Plan

Title:	**Lesson 21 - Nine-Patch Quilt**

Date:		Grade:	K-4

Suggested Season / Date: Winter / February, week 1

Time: 30 minutes (approx.)

Subject: Social Studies, Interdisciplinary Activities

Learning Style / Different Multiple Intelligences: Tactile/Kinesthetic; Visual/Spatial Intelligences (activity could be used for all areas)

Example: hands on, designing and creating a nine-patch quilt block

Materials Needed:

1) *The Long Winter*, pages 1-83
2) *My Little House Crafts Book*, pages 32-37 Adaptation
3) *The World of Little House*, pages 34-35
4) *Little House in the Classroom*, pages 105-106
5) *Activities for Elementary School Social Studies*, pages 7.10-7.11 Adaptation
6) *Little House Social Studies Curriculum Guide*, Activity, Performance Assessment Task, Student Scoring Guide, Teacher Scoring Guide: Lesson 21 - Nine-Patch Quilt

Introduction:

1) Read from *The Long Winter*.
2) Share resources about quilts and quilt-making. Display various patterns of quilts and quilt blocks.
3) The purpose is to introduce and to learn about sewing and quilt-making.

Little House Social Studies Curriculum Guide ©2005

Major Instructional Sequence:

4) Explain concept of quilt-making.
5) Model quilting a nine-patch quilt block.
6) Ask questions for understanding.

Concluding Sequence/Closure:

7) *Little House Social Studies Curriculum Guide*, Activity: Lesson 21 - Nine-Patch Quilt

Evaluation:

8) *Little House Social Studies Curriculum Guide*, Performance Assessment Task, Student Scoring Guide, Teacher Scoring Guide: Lesson 21 - Nine-Patch Quilt

Alignment to State Standards:

(compare to standards shown: Arkansas)

Strand 2:	People, Places and Environments
Content Standard 1:	Students will demonstrate an understanding that people, cultures and systems are connected and that commonalities and diversities exist among them.

Learning Expectations

PPE.1.1	Investigate how members of a family, school, community, state, nation and culture depend on each other.
PPE.1.2	Compare and contrast similarities and differences in cultures through a variety of experiences, such as reading, writing, drawing, role-playing, dance, music and simulation.
PPE.1.6	Distinguish similarities and differences among families and communities around the world.

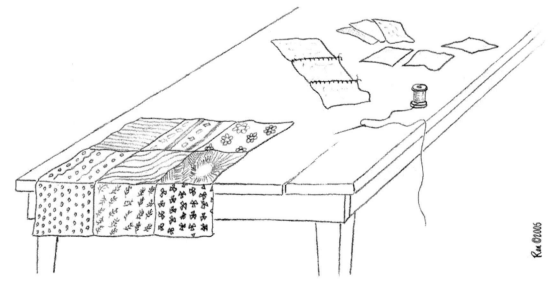

Activity

Title:	**Lesson 21 - Nine-Patch Quilt**

Sources:

1) *Activities for Elementary School Social Studies*, pages 7.10-7.11 Adaptation

Materials Needed:

1) five squares (each 4" x 4") printed cotton fabric (per student)
2) four squares (each 4" x 4") contrasting printed cotton fabric (per student)
3) white construction paper, glue, rulers

Objectives:

As a result of this activity, the student will:
o create a nine-patch quilt block
o understand that putting the blocks together forms a quilt
o know that the nine-patch pattern is named for the nine small squares sewn together

Introduction:

1) Show examples of nine-patch quilt block patterns.
2) Explain the meaning of nine-patch pattern.
3) Demonstrate the steps in forming the nine-patch pattern:
   a. deciding which prints go in what order
   b. cutting out appropriate sizes and print pieces
   c. gluing the pieces on the construction paper in the pattern decided upon

Major Instructional Sequence:

4) Student should obtain the needed materials.
5) Student will plan how to lay out the various pieces to form a pattern.
6) Allow work to begin, then circulate and offer helpful suggestions.

Concluding Sequence/Closure:

7) Each student will show their nine-patch quilt block.
8) Display nine-patch quilt blocks together, in an exhibit area, forming a nine-patch quilt.

Performance Assessment Task

Title:	**Lesson 21 - Nine-Patch Quilt**		

Name:		Grade:	K-4
Date:		Subject:	Social Studies

Alignment to State Standards:
(minimum of three standards, input State standards below)

Code	Standard Description

Description of Performance Task:
(include time, student performance, assessment)

Time:	30 minutes (approx.)
Activity:	Activity will correlate with reading *The Long Winter*.
Task:	o Student will state that a nine-patch pattern is named for the nine small squares sewn together. o Student will understand that putting blocks together forms a quilt. o Student will demonstrate the steps in forming the nine-patch pattern. o Student will distinguish between quilt patterns. o Student will display their nine-patch quilt block with the class, creating a nine-patch quilt.

Student Scoring Guide:	(attach a copy)

Teacher Scoring Guide:	(attach a copy of scoring key)
Score (select one):	[4] Exemplary [3] Proficient [2] Apprentice [1] Novice

Student Scoring Guide

Title: | **Lesson 21 - Nine-Patch Quilt**

Name:

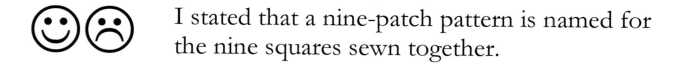 I stated that a nine-patch pattern is named for the nine squares sewn together.

😊😞 I understood that putting nine squares together forms a nine-patch quilt.

😊😞 I demonstrated the steps in forming the nine-patch pattern.

😊😞 I distinguished between quilt patterns.

😊😞 I displayed my nine-patch quilt block with the class, forming a quilt.

Little House Social Studies Curriculum Guide ©2005

Teacher Scoring Guide

Title: **Lesson 21 - Nine-Patch Quilt**

[4] Exemplary	o Effective validating that a nine-patch pattern is named for the nine small squares sewn together.
	o Contains few errors creating blocks to form a quilt.
	o Consistently devises a quilt pattern by piecing squares together.
	o Handles well exhibiting quilt blocks with other quilt blocks.

[3] Proficient	o Reasonably deduces that a nine-patch pattern is named for the nine small squares sewn together.
	o Ideas progress to demonstrate blocks to form a quilt.
	o Some weakness distinguishing a quilt pattern by piecing squares together.
	o Focuses on exhibiting quilt blocks with other quilt blocks.

[2] Apprentice	o Not too clear generalizing that a nine-patch pattern is named for the nine small squares sewn together.
	o Inconsistent in converting blocks to form a quilt.
	o Significant weakness discriminating a quilt pattern by piecing squares together.
	o No particular order in exhibiting quilt blocks with other quilt blocks.

[1] Novice	o Unclear identifying that a nine-patch pattern is named for the nine small squares sewn together.
	o Little or no selecting blocks to form a quilt.
	o Lacks in matching a quilt pattern by piecing squares together.
	o Serious errors in exhibiting quilt blocks with other quilt blocks.

Lesson Plan

Title:	**Lesson 22 - Snowflakes**

Date:		Grade:	K-4

Suggested Season / Date: Winter / February, week 2

Time: 30 minutes (approx.)

Subject: Social Studies, Anthropology Activities

Learning Style / Different Multiple Intelligences: Visual; Naturalistic Intelligence (activity could be used for all areas)

Example: seeing, geography, weather, learns best by study of natural phenomenon, snowflakes

Materials Needed:

1) *The Long Winter*, pages 84-166
2) *Little House in the Classroom*, pages 86-87
3) *Across the Curriculum with Favorite Authors*, pages 78-79
4) *Activities for Elementary School Social Studies*, pages 3.4-3.5 Adaptation
5) *Little House Social Studies Curriculum Guide*, Activity, Performance Assessment Task, Student Scoring Guide, Teacher Scoring Guide: Lesson 22 - Snowflakes

Introduction:

1) Read from *The Long Winter*.
2) Discover how each snowflake is different.
3) The purpose is to learn, compare and examine how each snowflake is different.

Major Instructional Sequence:

4) Look at visuals of snowflakes and hopefully watch real snowflakes.

Little House Social Studies Curriculum Guide ©2005

5) Model making a paper snowflake.
6) Check for understanding.

Concluding Sequence/Closure:

7) *Little House Social Studies Curriculum Guide*, Activity: Lesson 22 - Snowflakes

Evaluation:

8) *Little House Social Studies Curriculum Guide*, Performance Assessment Task, Student Scoring Guide, Teacher Scoring Guide: Lesson 22 - Snowflakes

Alignment to State Standards:

(compare to standards shown: Arkansas)

Strand 5:	Social Science Processes and Skills
Content Standard 1:	Students will demonstrate critical thinking skills through research, reading, writing, speaking, listening and problem-solving.

Learning Expectations

SSPS.1.3	Interpret information from visual aids, such as graphs and maps.
SSPS.1.5	Explore the concept of cause and effect.
SSPS.1.6	Compare, contrast and classify to recognize similarities and differences.

Activity

Title: **Lesson 22 - Snowflakes**

Sources:

1) *Activities for Elementary School Social Studies*, pages 3.4-3.5 Adaptation

Materials Needed:

1) snowflake pattern
2) blue construction paper
3) glue, scissors
4) white paper

Objectives:

As a result of this activity, the student will:
o create snowflakes using their own pattern and paper
o discover that each snowflake is different
o talk about the differences and similarities
o examine and compare different snowflakes side by side

Introduction:

1) Tell students to look at various pictures of snowflakes (and real ones if possible).
2) Talk about how they are alike and how they are different.
3) Tell students they will perform an activity to see the differences in their snowflakes.

Major Instructional Sequence:

4) Using art supplies (listed above):
    a. Make snowflakes using pattern.
    b. Glue on to blue construction paper.
5) Make a variety of extra snowflakes cutting out white paper.
6) Display the snowflakes, hanging the extra snowflakes above students' desks.
7) Lead students in a discussion of how the snowflakes are different.

Concluding Sequence/Closure:

8) Each student will display their snowflakes.
9) Students will view the extra snowflakes hanging above their desks.

Performance Assessment Task

Title: **Lesson 22 - Snowflakes**

Name:

Date:

Grade: K-4

Subject: Social Studies

Alignment to State Standards:
(minimum of three standards, input State standards below)

Code	Standard Description

Description of Performance Task:
(include time, student performance, assessment)

Time:	30 minutes (approx.)
Activity:	Activity will correlate with reading *The Long Winter*.
Task:	o Student will look at pictures of snowflakes and observe the difference.
	o Student will produce a snowflake using the pattern.
	o Student will glue snowflake on blue construction paper.
	o Student will make extra snowflakes cutting out their own design on white paper.
	o Student will display snowflake and hang extra snowflakes above their desk.
	o Student will share about how each snowflake is different.
	o Student will observe real snowflakes falling from the sky, if possible.

Student Scoring Guide: (attach a copy)

Teacher Scoring Guide: (attach a copy of scoring key)

Score (select one): [4] Exemplary [3] Proficient [2] Apprentice [1] Novice

Student Scoring Guide

Title: 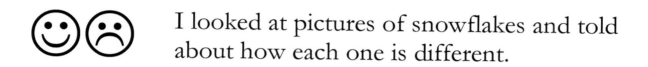 **Lesson 22 - Snowflakes**

Name:

☺ ☹   I looked at pictures of snowflakes and told about how each one is different.

☺ ☹   I discovered how each snowflake is different by comparing them.

☺ ☹   I produced a snowflake using the snowflake pattern and glued it on blue construction paper.

☺ ☹   I differentiated between snowflakes from cutting out extra snowflakes using white paper.

☺ ☹   I displayed my snowflakes hanging overhead.

Little House Social Studies Curriculum Guide ©2005

Teacher Scoring Guide

Title: | **Lesson 22 - Snowflakes**

---

[4] Exemplary
- o Effective contrasting between snowflakes.
- o Consistently produces extra snowflakes by cutting out of white paper.
- o Fluently shares about the differences of each snowflake.
- o Handles well displaying snowflake and has snowflakes hanging overhead.

---

[3] Proficient
- o Clearly distinguishes between snowflakes.
- o Appropriately produces extra snowflakes by cutting out of white paper.
- o Reasonably differentiates the differences of each snowflake.
- o Fairly strong display of snowflake and has snowflakes hanging overhead.

---

[2] Apprentice
- o Inconsistently summarizes between snowflakes.
- o Not elaborately produces extra snowflakes by cutting out of white paper.
- o No particular discriminating the differences of each snowflake.
- o Basic display of snowflake and has snowflakes hanging overhead.

---

[1] Novice
- o Little or no describing between snowflakes.
- o Lacks in producing extra snowflakes by cutting out of white paper.
- o Random labeling the differences of each snowflake.
- o Serious errors in displaying snowflake and has snowflakes hanging overhead.

Lesson Plan

Title:	**Lesson 23 - Distinguish Wants & Needs**

Date:		Grade:	K-4

Suggested Season / Date: Winter / February, week 3

Time: 30 minutes (approx.)

Subject: Social Studies, Economics Activities

Learning Style / Different Multiple Intelligences: Tactile/Kinesthetic; Interpersonal Intelligence (activity could be used for all areas)

Example: hands on, touching, doing, making charts, posters, cooperate as a group

Materials Needed:

1) *The Long Winter*, pages 167-249
2) *Little House in the Classroom*, pages 84-85
3) *The World of Little House*, pages 74-78
4) *Across the Curriculum with Favorite Authors*, pages 76, 79
5) *Activities for Elementary School Social Studies*, pages 5.3-5.4
6) *Little House Social Studies Curriculum Guide*, Activity, Performance Assessment Task, Student Scoring Guide, Teacher Scoring Guide: Lesson 23 - Distinguish Wants & Needs

Introduction:

1) Read from *The Long Winter*.
2) Share information about what Laura's family needed to survive.
3) The purpose is to learn between needs and wants.

   Little House Social Studies Curriculum Guide ©2005

Major Instructional Sequence:

4) Discuss differences between needs and wants. Explain concept of what it took for the Ingalls to survive the blizzards.
5) Allow time for questions about what we need and what we want.
6) Check for understanding.

Concluding Sequence/Closure:

7) *Little House Social Studies Curriculum Guide*, Activity: Lesson 23 - Distinguish Wants & Needs

Evaluation:

8) *Little House Social Studies Curriculum Guide*, Performance Assessment Task, Student Scoring Guide, Teacher Scoring Guide: Lesson 23 - Distinguish Wants & Needs

Alignment to State Standards:

(compare to standards shown: Arkansas)

Strand 3:	Production, Distribution and Consumption
Content Standard 1:	Students will demonstrate an understanding that different economic systems and limited resources influence cooperation and conflict in decisions.

Learning Expectations

PDC.1.1	Categorize and prioritize wants and needs.
PDC.1.6	Examine how people depend on each other to supply economic goods and services.
PDC.1.7	Recognize different means of economic exchange.

Activity

Title:	**Lesson 23 - Distinguish Wants & Needs**

Sources:

1) *Activities for Elementary School Social Studies*, pages 5.3-5.4

Materials Needed:

1) magazines, newspapers, advertising brochures
2) poster board
3) scissors, glue
4) marking pens

Objectives:

As a result of this activity, the student will:
o distinguish between wants and needs
o select ads depicting wants; select ads depicting needs
o make collages of wants and needs with pictures from advertisements

Introduction:

1) Make headings for two columns on the chalkboard, one labeled WANTS and one labeled NEEDS.
2) Brainstorm with students about kinds of things that might be placed under each.

Major Instructional Sequence:

3) Divide students into cooperative work groups.
4) Supply each group with poster board, magazines, newspapers, etc.
5) Have groups go through the magazines, newspaper, etc, looking for ads showing things that could be classified as either WANTS or NEEDS.
6) Students are to cut out the pictures, work cooperatively to categorize them and glue them in a collage on the appropriate (either WANTS or NEEDS) poster board.

Concluding Sequence/Closure:

7) Groups show their posters and identify the advertisements depicting WANTS and the advertisements depicting NEEDS.
8) Display completed WANTS and NEEDS posters.

Performance Assessment Task

Title:	**Lesson 23 - Distinguish Wants & Needs**

Name:		Grade:	K-4
Date:		Subject:	Social Studies

Alignment to State Standards:
(minimum of three standards, input State standards below)

Code	Standard Description

Description of Performance Task:
(include time, student performance, assessment)

Time:	30 minutes (approx.)
Activity:	Activity will correlate with reading *The Long Winter*.
Task:	o Student will identify wants and needs. o Student will distinguish between wants and needs. o Student will use pictures from magazines, newspapers and advertisement brochures to classify wants and needs. o Student will differentiate between wants and needs in a collage on poster board. o Student will display wants and needs poster.

Student Scoring Guide: (attach a copy)

Teacher Scoring Guide: (attach a copy of scoring key)

Score (select one): [4] Exemplary [3] Proficient [2] Apprentice [1] Novice

Student Scoring Guide

Title: **Lesson 23 - Distinguish Wants & Needs**

Name:

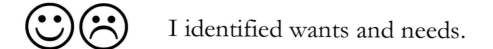 I identified wants and needs.

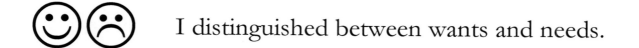 I distinguished between wants and needs.

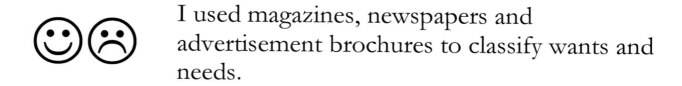 I used magazines, newspapers and advertisement brochures to classify wants and needs.

I differentiated between wants and needs in a collage on poster board.

I displayed my wants and needs poster.

Little House Social Studies Curriculum Guide ©2005

Teacher Scoring Guide

Title: | **Lesson 23 - Distinguish Wants & Needs**

---

[4] Exemplary
- o Effectively interprets wants and needs.
- o Clearly formulates differences between wants and needs.
- o Handles well justifying pictures from magazines, newspapers and advertisement brochures of wants and needs.
- o Contains few errors displaying wants and needs on poster.

---

[3] Proficient
- o Reasonably deduces wants and needs.
- o Focuses on distinguishing differences between wants and needs.
- o Fairly strong in differentiating pictures from magazines, newspapers and advertisement brochures of wants and needs.
- o Appropriately displays wants and needs on poster.

---

[2] Apprentice
- o Inconsistent inference of wants and needs.
- o Weak progression explaining differences between wants and needs.
- o Repetitive distinguishing of pictures from magazines, newspapers and advertisement brochures of wants and needs.
- o No particular order to display of wants and needs on poster.

---

[1] Novice
- o Little or no naming of wants and needs.
- o Very little labeling differences between wants and needs.
- o Unclear listing of pictures from magazines, newspapers and advertisement brochures of wants and needs.
- o Random display of wants and needs on poster.

Lesson Plan

Title:	**Lesson 24 - Wood Whittling**

Date:		Grade:	K-4

Suggested Season / Date: | Winter / February, week 4

Time: | 30 minutes (approx.)

Subject: | Social Studies, Anthropology Activities

Learning Style / Different Multiple Intelligences: | Tactile/Kinesthetic; Naturalistic Intelligence (activity could be used for all areas)

Example: | hands on, touching, doing, interact with surroundings and learning how things work using wood, sweet potatoes

Materials Needed:

1) *The Long Winter*, pages 250-334
2) *The World of Little House*, pages 74-78
3) *Activities for Elementary School Social Studies*, pages 3.2-3.3 Adaptation
4) *Little House Social Studies Curriculum Guide*, Activity, Performance Assessment Task, Student Scoring Guide, Teacher Scoring Guide: Lesson 24 - Wood Whittling

Introduction:

1) Read from *The Long Winter*.
2) Share information about carving objects by whittling wood.
3) The purpose is to learn about whittling and creating wood carvings.

Major Instructional Sequence:

4) Discuss the art of whittling wood and creating wood carvings.
5) Examine pictures of wood carvings in encyclopedias, picture dictionaries and illustrated informational books.

6) Ask questions for understanding about wood whittling.

Concluding Sequence/Closure:

7) *Little House Social Studies Curriculum Guide*, Activity: Lesson 24 - Wood Whittling

Evaluation:

8) *Little House Social Studies Curriculum Guide*, Performance Assessment Task, Student Scoring Guide, Teacher Scoring Guide: Lesson 24 - Wood Whittling

Alignment to State Standards:

(compare to standards shown: Arkansas)

Strand 1:	Time, Continuity and Change
Content Standard 2:	Students will demonstrate an understanding of how ideas, events and conditions bring about change.

Learning Expectations

TCC.2.1	Discuss and record changes in one's self, community, state and nation.
TCC.2.4	Explain how people, places, events, tools, institutions, attitudes, values and ideas are the result of what has one before.
TCC.2.5	Use a variety of processes, such as thinking, reading, writing, listening and speaking, to demonstrate continuity and change.

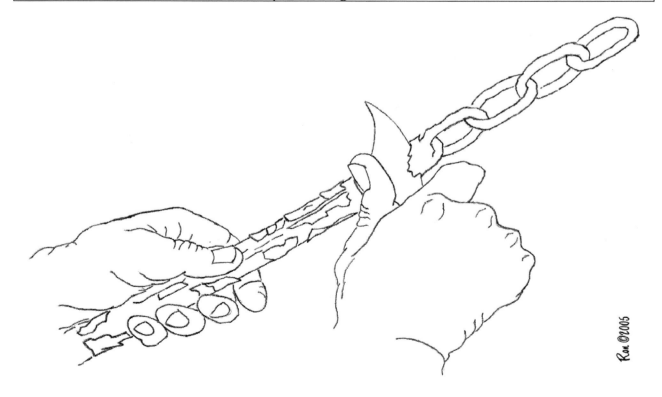

Ron ©2005

Activity

Title: | **Lesson 24 - Wood Whittling**

Sources:

1) *Activities for Elementary School Social Studies*, pages 3.2-3.3 Adaptation

Materials Needed:

1) raw sweet potatoes
2) plastic knives, popsicle sticks
3) butcher paper
4) picture books with good illustrations of wood carvings, picture dictionaries and encyclopedias

Objectives:

As a result of this activity, the student will:
o practice fine motor skills
o have fun while whittling out a sweet potato
o enhance sensory awareness
o develop knowledge of whittling wood

Introduction:

1) Tell students about how people whittled out wood years ago.
2) Examine pictures of wood carvings from long ago, in picture books, encyclopedias and picture dictionaries and illustrated informational books. Call attention to carvings made out of wood.
3) Tell students that they will make their own carving, whittling sweet potatoes.

Major Instructional Sequence:

4) Set up work areas around the room with the necessary supplies.
5) Model using a plastic knife to design a carving using a sweet potato.
6) Provide each student with a section of butcher paper.
7) Students place the sweet potato carving on the butcher paper to dry out.

Concluding Sequence/Closure:

8) Each student shows and tells about his/her sweet potato carving.
9) Display the sweet potato carvings.

Little House Social Studies Curriculum Guide ©2005

Performance Assessment Task

Title:	**Lesson 24 - Wood Whittling**

Name:		Grade:	K-4
Date:		Subject:	Social Studies

Alignment to State Standards:
(minimum of three standards, input State standards below)

Code	Standard Description

Description of Performance Task:
(include time, student performance, assessment)

Time:	30 minutes (approx.)
Activity:	Activity will correlate with reading *The Long Winter*.
Task:	o Student will tell about what a wood carving is. o Student will investigate pictures of wood carvings using reference materials. o Student will practice wood whittling by whittling a sweet potato using a plastic knife. o Student will differentiate between wood carvings. o Student will display the sweet potato carving.

Student Scoring Guide: | (attach a copy) |

Teacher Scoring Guide: | (attach a copy of scoring key) |
Score (select one): | [4] Exemplary [3] Proficient [2] Apprentice [1] Novice |

Student Scoring Guide

Title: **Lesson 24 - Wood Whittling**

Name:

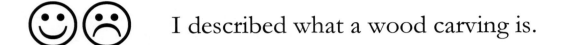 I described what a wood carving is.

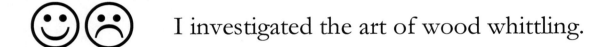 I investigated the art of wood whittling.

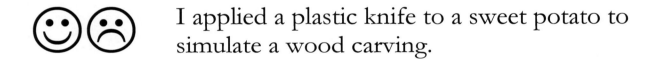 I applied a plastic knife to a sweet potato to simulate a wood carving.

 I differentiated between wood carvings.

I displayed my sweet potato carving.

Teacher Scoring Guide

Title: **Lesson 24 - Wood Whittling**

[4] Exemplary
- o Clearly addresses and concludes what a wood carving is.
- o Effective investigating about the art of wood whittling.
- o Consistent whittling with a plastic knife a sweet potato carving.
- o Contains few errors displaying a sweet potato carving.

[3] Proficient
- o Focuses on relating to what a wood carving is.
- o Some errors deducing the art of wood whittling.
- o Reasonable whittling with a plastic knife a sweet potato carving.
- o Appropriately displays a sweet potato carving.

[2] Apprentice
- o Inconsistent explaining about what a wood carving is.
- o Weak progression discussing about the art of wood whittling.
- o Many errors whittling with a plastic knife a sweet potato carving.
- o Basically displays a sweet potato carving.

[1] Novice
- o Unclear naming of what a wood carving is.
- o Little or no defining about the art of wood whittling.
- o Little or no whittling with a plastic knife a sweet potato carving.
- o Random display of a sweet potato carving.

Lesson Plan

Title:	**Lesson 25 - Making a Flag Cake**
Date:	Grade: K-4
Suggested Season / Date:	Spring / March, week 1
Time:	30 minutes (approx.)
Subject:	Social Studies, Political Science Activities
Learning Style / Different Multiple Intelligences:	Tactile/Kinesthetic; Interpersonal Intelligence (activity could be used for all areas)
Example:	hands on, doing, creating and designing a flag cake as a group

Materials Needed:

1) *Little Town on the Prairie*, pages 1-77
2) *Little House in the Classroom*, pages 95-97
3) *The World of Little House*, pages 90-92
4) *Across the Curriculum with Favorite Authors*, pages 88-89
5) *Activities for Elementary School Social Studies*, pages 6.2-6.3
6) *Little House Social Studies Curriculum Guide*, Activity, Performance Assessment Task, Student Scoring Guide, Teacher Scoring Guide: Lesson 25 - Making a Flag Cake

Introduction:

1) Read from *Little Town on the Prairie*.
2) Share information about celebrating Independence Day.
3) The purpose is to learn about celebrating Independence Day.

Major Instructional Sequence:

4) Provide pictures and information about Independence Day.

5) Explain concepts about how Laura's family celebrated and how we celebrate. State definitions concerning Independence Day.
6) Provide examples of celebrating Independence Day.
7) Check for understanding through posing key questions.

Concluding Sequence/Closure:

8) *Little House Social Studies Curriculum Guide*, Activity: Lesson 25 - Making a Flag Cake

Evaluation:

9) *Little House Social Studies Curriculum Guide*, Performance Assessment Task, Student Scoring Guide, Teacher Scoring Guide: Lesson 25 - Making a Flag Cake

Alignment to State Standards:

(compare to standards shown: Arkansas)

Strand 4:	Power, Authority and Governance
Content Standard 1:	Students will demonstrate an understanding of the ideals, right and responsibilities of participating in a democratic society.

Learning Expectations

PAG.1.1	Explain the need for rules or laws in home, school, community, state and nation.
PAG.1.2	Exhibit an understanding of the rights and responsibilities of citizenship in the community, nation.
PAG.1.6	Use a variety of processes, such as thinking, reading, writing, speaking, listening and role playing, to promote responsible citizenship.

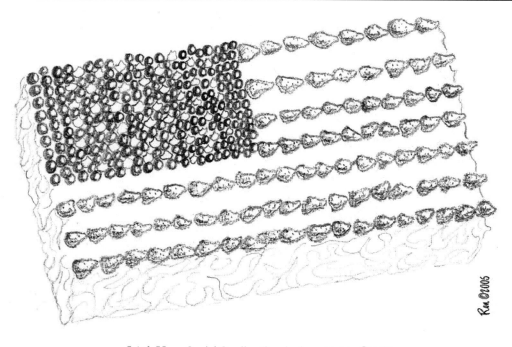

Activity

Title:

Lesson 25 - Making a Flag Cake

Sources:

1) *Activities for Elementary School Social Studies*, pages 6.2-6.3

Materials Needed:

1) U.S. flag
2) pictures and picture books of the U.S. flag
3) white cakes (previously prepared) in 13" x 9" pans
4) bowls of sliced strawberries and blueberries
5) whipped topping
6) cake knife, plastic forks, paper plates, napkins

Objectives:

As a result of this activity, the student will:
o decorate flat cakes to resemble the U.S. flag
o know that stars stand for states in the U.S.
o know that stripes stand for the first thirteen colonies established in the U.S.

Introduction:

1) Show the flag of the U.S.
2) Arrange flag pictures and picture books on a table for students to examine.
3) Tell students they will decorate a cake to look like the flag.

Major Instructional Sequence:

4) Divide students in groups and have cakes / materials located on different tables.
5) Show how to ice a cake with whipped topping and let students perform the task.
6) Demonstrate how to place the blueberries, leaving spaces of white to represent the stars on the flag. Let students place the blueberries.
7) Demonstrate how to place the strawberries to represent the red stripes on the flag. Have students place the strawberries.

Concluding Sequence/Closure:

8) Let everyone walk around to view all of the cakes.
9) Take pictures of each group with their cake before letting them eat the cakes.

Little House Social Studies Curriculum Guide ©2005

Performance Assessment Task

Title: **Lesson 25 - Making a Flag Cake**

Name: | Grade: | K-4

Date: | Subject: | Social Studies

Alignment to State Standards:
(minimum of three standards, input State standards below)

Code	Standard Description

Description of Performance Task:
(include time, student performance, assessment)

Time:	30 minutes (approx.)
Activity:	Activity will correlate with reading *Little Town on the Prairie*.
Task:	o Student will describe the United States flag. o Student will demonstrate, along with a group, understanding of the United States flag using a white cake, whipped topping, strawberries and blueberries. o Student will differentiate between the different parts of the United States flag. o Student will display, along with a group, the flag cake for pictures and then enjoy eating the flag cake.

Student Scoring Guide: | (attach a copy)

Teacher Scoring Guide: | (attach a copy of scoring key)

Score (select one): | [4] Exemplary [3] Proficient [2] Apprentice [1] Novice

Student Scoring Guide

Title: | **Lesson 25 - Making a Flag Cake**

Name:

😊😞 I described the United States flag.

😊😞 I discussed the meaning of the stars and the stripes on the flag.

😊😞 I demonstrated the flag using white cake, whipped topping, blueberries and strawberries.

😊😞 I differentiated about the different parts of the flag.

😊😞 I displayed, along with my group, the flag cake for pictures and then enjoyed eating the flag cake.

Little House Social Studies Curriculum Guide ©2005

Teacher Scoring Guide

Title: | **Lesson 25 - Making a Flag Cake**

[4] Exemplary
- Clearly addresses formulating about the United States flag.
- Effectively creates a flag cake (with a group) using a white cake, whipped topping, strawberries and blueberries.
- Consistently differentiates parts of the United States flag.
- Handles well displaying the flag cake for pictures before eating the flag cake.

[3] Proficient
- Reasonably deduces about the United States flag.
- Focuses on preparing a flag cake (with a group) using a white cake, whipped topping, strawberries and blueberries.
- Appropriately relates about parts of the United States flag.
- Fairly strong display of the flag cake for pictures before eating the flag cake.

[2] Apprentice
- Not clear explaining about the United States flag.
- Significant weakness converting a flag cake (with a group) using a white cake, whipped topping, strawberries and blueberries.
- Inconsistent summarizing about parts of the United States flag.
- Not focused on displaying the flag cake for pictures before eating the flag cake.

[1] Novice
- Little or no identifying about the United States flag.
- Random outlining a flag cake (with a group) using a white cake, whipped topping, strawberries and blueberries.
- Impeded matching about parts of the United States flag.
- Serious errors displaying the flag cake for pictures before eating the flag cake.

Lesson Plan

Title:	**Lesson 26 - Autograph Album**

Date:		Grade:	K-4

Suggested Season / Date:	Spring / March, week 2

Time:	30 minutes (approx.)

Subject:	Social Studies, Sociology Activities

Learning Style / Different Multiple Intelligences:	Tactile/Kinesthetic; Intrapersonal Intelligence (activity could be used for all areas)

Example:	hands on, moving, touching and doing writing and having their own space writing messages on an autograph album

Materials Needed:

1) *Little Town on the Prairie*, pages 78-154
2) *Across the Curriculum with Favorite Authors*, pages 90-99
3) *The World of Little House*, pages 93-94
4) *Activities for Elementary School Social Studies*, pages 4.18-4.19 Adaptation
5) *Little House Social Studies Curriculum Guide*, Activity, Performance Assessment Task, Student Scoring Guide, Teacher Scoring Guide: Lesson 26 - Autograph Album

Introduction:

1) Read from *Little Town on the Prairie*.
2) Share information about an autograph album. Discuss how family, friends and classmates write messages.
3) The purpose is to create an autograph album.

Major Instructional Sequence:

4) Provide information about writing in an autograph album. Explain concepts about how the autograph albums were considered fashionable.

5) State definitions for an autograph album.
6) Provide examples of autograph albums.
7) Check for understanding.

Concluding Sequence/Closure:

8) *Little House Social Studies Curriculum Guide*, Activity: Lesson 26 - Autograph Album

Evaluation:

9) *Little House Social Studies Curriculum Guide*, Performance Assessment Task, Student Scoring Guide, Teacher Scoring Guide: Lesson 26 - Autograph Album

Alignment to State Standards:

(compare to standards shown: Arkansas)

Strand 5:	Social Science Processes and Skills
Content Standard 2:	Students will demonstrate the ability to use the tools of the social sciences.
Learning Expectations	
SSPS.2.1	Define and apply key features on maps and globes.
SSPS.2.2	Identify and use primary and secondary sources, such as photographs, documents, letters, diaries, stories and field studies.
SSPS.2.3	Utilize interactive technologies.

Activity

Title: | **Lesson 26 - Autograph Album**

Sources:

1) *Activities for Elementary School Social Studies*, pages 4.18-4.19 Adaptation

Materials Needed:

1) construction paper or card stock
2) pastel-colored paper; two sheets each of three or four colors
3) scissors, ruler, hole punch and pen
4) narrow ribbons or cords, about 12" long

Objectives:

As a result of this activity, the student will:
o participate in an intrapersonal activity to produce an autograph album
o write a message and autographs for a classmate in their autograph album

Introduction:

1) Talk about how useful and nice it would be to have an autograph album from your friends and family.
2) Let students examine an autograph album from a previous class.
3) Tell students they will make an autograph album.

Major Instructional Sequence:

4) Let students begin constructing autograph album.
5) Circulate and check for understanding, giving assistance.
6) Have each student write on the page of another classmate.
7) Help students to work cooperatively so each student gets a turn to write a message and autograph.

Concluding Sequence/Closure:

8) Let each student read a page.
9) Place the autograph albums in a place where they may be easily examined by classmates and visitors.

Little House Social Studies Curriculum Guide ©2005

Performance Assessment Task

Title: **Lesson 26 - Autograph Album**

Name: Grade: K-4

Date: Subject: Social Studies

Alignment to State Standards:
(minimum of three standards, input State standards below)

Code	Standard Description

Description of Performance Task:
(include time, student performance, assessment)

Time: 30 minutes (approx.)

Activity: Activity will correlate with reading *Little Town on the Prairie*.

Task:
- Student will recall how Laura and friends used an autograph album.
- Student will discuss how useful and nice it would be to have signatures and messages from friends and family.
- Student will use card stock, colored paper and art tools to construct an autograph album.
- Student will create and design an autograph album.
- Student will sign and write messages in classmates' albums.
- Student will share a message and display their autograph album.

Student Scoring Guide: (attach a copy)

Teacher Scoring Guide: (attach a copy of scoring key)

Score (select one): [4] Exemplary [3] Proficient [2] Apprentice [1] Novice

Student Scoring Guide

Title: **Lesson 26 - Autograph Album**

Name:

😊😞 I told about how Laura and friends used an autograph album.

😊😞 I discussed how useful and nice it would be to have messages from family and friends.

😊😞 I used card stock, colored paper and art tools to construct my autograph album.

😊😞 I created and designed my own autograph album.

😊😞 I shared a message and displayed my autograph album.

Little House Social Studies Curriculum Guide ©2005

Teacher Scoring Guide

Title: | **Lesson 26 - Autograph Album**

[4] Exemplary	o Fluently interprets how Laura and her friends used an autograph album.
	o Clearly addresses and compares how useful and fun it is to have signatures and messages from friends and family.
	o Handles well designing and creating an autograph album using art tools.
	o Effectively summarizes a selected message to share with the class.

[3] Proficient	o Reasonably differentiates how Laura and her friends used an autograph album.
	o Clearly relates how useful and fun it is to have signatures and messages from friends and family.
	o Appropriately formulates an autograph album using art tools.
	o Fairly strong outline of a selected message to share with the class.

[2] Apprentice	o Lacks evidence of explaining how Laura and friends used an autograph album.
	o Contains some sense of how useful and fun it is to have signatures and messages from friends and family.
	o Contains errors distinguishing an autograph album using art tools.
	o Not much information paraphrasing a selected message to share with the class.

[1] Novice	o Little or no naming of how Laura and her friends used an autograph album.
	o Sparse recollection of how useful and fun it is to have signatures and messages from friends and family.
	o Serious errors labeling an autograph album using art tools.
	o Unclear describing of a selected message to share with the class.

Lesson Plan

Title:	**Lesson 27 - Paper Dolls**

Date:		Grade:	K-4

Suggested Season / Date:	Spring / March, week 3

Time:	30 minutes (approx.)

Subject:	Social Studies

Learning Style / Different Multiple Intelligences:	Tactile/Kinesthetic; Visual/Spatial Intelligence (activity could be used for all areas)

Example:	hands on, doing and touching, creating and designing paper dolls

Materials Needed:

1) *Little Town on the Prairie*, pages 155-230
2) *Across the Curriculum with Favorite Authors*, pages 90-98
3) *The World of Little House*, pages 87-92
4) *Activities for Elementary School Social Studies*, page 2.23 Adaptation
5) *Little House Social Studies Curriculum Guide*, Activity, Performance Assessment Task, Student Scoring Guide, Teacher Scoring Guide: Lesson 27 - Paper Dolls

Introduction:

1) Read from *Little Town on the Prairie*.
2) Discuss history of dolls and use reference materials.
3) The purpose is to learn about making paper dolls.

Major Instructional Sequence:

4) Provide information using reference materials, catalogs, magazines and various dolls.

5) Discuss various kinds of dolls now and then. Search reference materials looking at various kinds of dolls and display various kinds of dolls. Talk about what Laura would have had available to her.

6) Ask questions for understanding.

Concluding Sequence/Closure:

7) *Little House Social Studies Curriculum Guide*, Activity: Lesson 27 - Paper Dolls

Evaluation:

8) *Little House Social Studies Curriculum Guide*, Performance Assessment Task, Student Scoring Guide, Teacher Scoring Guide: Lesson 27 - Paper Dolls

Alignment to State Standards:

(compare to standards shown: Arkansas)

Strand 1:	Time, Continuity and Change
Content Standard 2:	Students will demonstrate an understanding of how ideas, events and conditions bring about change.

Learning Expectations

TCC.2.1	Discuss and record changes in one's self, community, state and nation.
TCC.2.3	Use personal experiences, biographies, autobiographies or historical fiction to explain how individuals are affected by, can cope with and can create change.
TCC.2.5	Use a variety of processes, such as thinking, reading, writing, listening and speaking, to demonstrate continuity and change.

Activity

Title: | **Lesson 27 - Paper Dolls**

Sources:

1) *Activities for Elementary School Social Studies*, page 2.23 Adaptation

Materials Needed:

1) magazines, catalogs
2) paper doll patterns
3) scissors
4) pictures, reference materials
5) various kinds of dolls for display

Objectives:

As a result of this activity, the student will:
o understand the significance of paper dolls in history
o utilize reference materials to learn about various kinds of dolls.
o produce paper dolls

Introduction:

1) Discuss and review life with various kinds of dolls.
2) Show pictures, magazines and catalogs with pictures of people.
3) Demonstrate different kinds of dolls, then and now.

Major Instructional Sequence:

4) Have students search magazines, catalogs and reference materials to look at different kinds of dolls.
5) Students are to cut out paper dolls. Students may begin by cutting out pictures of people in magazines and catalogs, then cut out paper doll patterns, color and dress them. Also, coloring and cutting out dress clothes for the paper dolls.
6) To add realism, students may make miniature wagons, trees and animals.

Concluding Sequence/Closure:

7) Students show their paper dolls to the class.
8) Students tell about their paper dolls to the class.
9) Students make a display of their paper dolls.

Little House Social Studies Curriculum Guide ©2005

Performance Assessment Task

Title: **Lesson 27 - Paper Dolls**

Name:

Date:

Grade: K-4

Subject: Social Studies

Alignment to State Standards:
(minimum of three standards, input State standards below)

Code	Standard Description

Description of Performance Task:
(include time, student performance, assessment)

Time: 30 minutes (approx.)

Activity: Activity will correlate with reading *Little Town on the Prairie.*

Task:
- Student will name and list various kinds of paper dolls.
- Student will search magazines, catalogs and paper doll patterns.
- Student will use a variety of paper doll patterns and art tools to demonstrate paper dolls.
- Student will create and design paper dolls and paper doll clothes.
- Student will share the paper dolls and paper doll clothes.
- Student will display the paper dolls and paper doll clothes.

Student Scoring Guide: (attach a copy)

Teacher Scoring Guide: (attach a copy of scoring key)

Score (select one): [4] Exemplary [3] Proficient [2] Apprentice [1] Novice

Student Scoring Guide

Title: | **Lesson 27 - Paper Dolls**

Name:

☺☹ I named and listed various kinds of paper dolls.

☺☹ I searched out pictures in magazines, catalogs and paper doll patterns.

☺☹ I used a variety of paper doll patterns and art tools to demonstrate paper dolls.

☺☹ I created and designed paper dolls and paper doll clothes.

☺☹ I shared and displayed my paper dolls and doll clothes.

Little House Social Studies Curriculum Guide ©2005

Teacher Scoring Guide

Title: **Lesson 27 - Paper Dolls**

[4] Exemplary	o Effectively concludes about various kinds of paper dolls.
	o Contains few errors compiling paper doll pictures and patterns.
	o Consistently creates and designs paper dolls and paper doll clothes.
	o Handles well sharing and displaying paper dolls and paper doll clothes.

[3] Proficient	o Reasonably relates about various kinds of paper dolls.
	o Focuses on organizing paper doll pictures and patterns.
	o Appropriately prepares paper dolls and paper doll clothes.
	o Some errors illustrating and displaying paper dolls and paper doll clothes.

[2] Apprentice	o Inconsistent distinguishing between various kinds of paper dolls.
	o Repetitive converting paper doll pictures and patterns.
	o Not clear putting together paper dolls and paper doll clothes.
	o Significant weakness naming and displaying paper dolls and paper doll clothes.

[1] Novice	o Unclear naming and listing various kinds of paper dolls.
	o Random matching paper doll pictures and patterns.
	o Serious errors selecting paper dolls and paper doll clothes.
	o Little or no identifying and displaying paper dolls and paper doll clothes.

Lesson Plan

Title:	**Lesson 28 - Spelling Bee**

Date:		Grade:	K-4

Suggested Season / Date: | Spring / March, week 4

Time: | 30 minutes (approx.)

Subject: | Social Studies / Political Science Activities

Learning Style / Different Multiple Intelligences: | Auditory; Verbal Linguistic Intelligence (activity could be used for all areas)

Example: | verbal, reading words aloud, listening and ability to spell words

Materials Needed:

1) *Little Town on the Prairie*, pages 231-307
2) *Across the Curriculum with Favorite Authors*, page 91
3) *The World of Little House*, pages 88-89
4) *Activities for Elementary School Social Studies*, pages 6.17-6.18 Adaptation
5) *Little House Social Studies Curriculum Guide*, Activity, Performance Assessment Task, Student Scoring Guide, Teacher Scoring Guide: Lesson 28 - Spelling Bee

Introduction:

1) Read from *Little Town on the Prairie*.
2) Share information about participating in Literaries.
3) The purpose is to participate in a Literary by having a Spelling Bee.

Major Instructional Sequence:

4) Explain concept of the community participating in Literaries.
5) Provide examples of participating in a Literary.
6) Check for understanding of Literaries and Spelling Bee.

Concluding Sequence/Closure:

7) *Little House Social Studies Curriculum Guide*, Activity: Lesson 28 - Spelling Bee

Evaluation:

8) *Little House Social Studies Curriculum Guide*, Performance Assessment Task, Student Scoring Guide, Teacher Scoring Guide: Lesson 28 - Spelling Bee

Alignment to State Standards:

(compare to standards shown: Arkansas)

Strand 5:	Social Science Processes and Skills
Content Standard 1:	Students will demonstrate critical thinking skills through research, reading, writing, speaking, listening and problem-solving.

Learning Expectations

SSPS.1.1	Communicate knowledge and ideas in a variety of forms, such as reports, persuasive essays, journals, news articles, graphic displays, speeches, videos and stories.
SSPS.1.4	Distinguish between fact and opinion.
SSPS.1.6	Compare, contrast and classify to recognize similarities and differences.

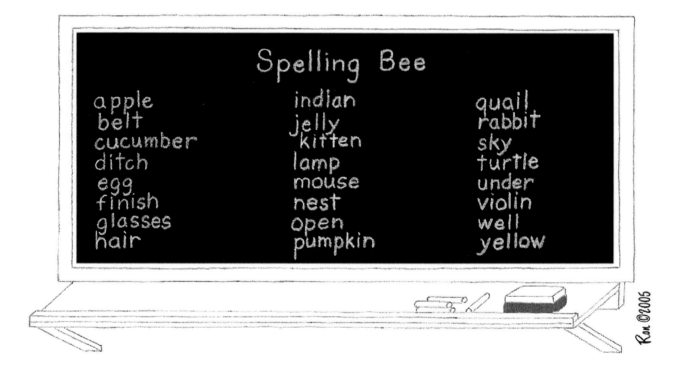

Activity

Title: | **Lesson 28 - Spelling Bee**

Sources:

1) *Activities for Elementary School Social Studies*, pages 6.17-6.18 Adaptation

Materials Needed:

1) spelling word list
2) student participants
3) teacher to pronounce words and give word lists

Objectives:

As a result of this activity, the student will:
o practice the spelling list
o participate in a Literary, a Spelling Bee
o understand competition of spell-down

Introduction:

1) Ask students to brainstorm ideas to use at a Literary meeting.
2) List ideas on the board for a Literary meeting as reading poetry, singing and other challenges.
3) Give examples of ways that people participate in Literaries in history.
4) Tell the class they are going to participate in a Spelling Bee.

Major Instructional Sequence:

5) After going over the spelling list together, have students line up in row to participate in the Spelling Bee.
6) Give opportunity for each student to participate in the spell-down.
7) Hold the Spelling Bee until there is a spelling winner.

Concluding Sequence/Closure:

8) At the end of Spelling Bee, there will be a winner.
9) Each student will understand the purpose of the Spelling Bee to be fluent with the spelling words.

Performance Assessment Task

Title:	**Lesson 28 - Spelling Bee**		
Name:		Grade:	K-4
Date:		Subject:	Social Studies

Alignment to State Standards:
(minimum of three standards, input State standards below)

Code	Standard Description

Description of Performance Task:
(include time, student performance, assessment)

Time:	30 minutes (approx.)
Activity:	Activity will correlate with reading *Little Town on the Prairie*.
Task:	o Student will name and list what a Literary is including a Spelling Bee. o Student will understand concept of participating in Literaries as a Spelling Bee. o Student will participate in a Spelling Bee, using words from a spelling list. o Student will synthesize and be more fluent at the spelling word list. o Student will perform in a Spelling Bee with others until there is a winner.

Student Scoring Guide: (attach a copy)

Teacher Scoring Guide: (attach a copy of scoring key)

Score (select one): [4] Exemplary [3] Proficient [2] Apprentice [1] Novice

Student Scoring Guide

Title: **Lesson 28 - Spelling Bee**

Name:

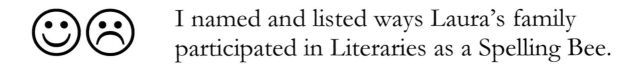 I named and listed ways Laura's family participated in Literaries as a Spelling Bee.

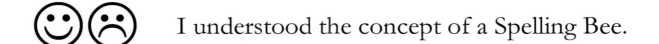 I understood the concept of a Spelling Bee.

I participated in a Spelling Bee, using words from a list, with others in my class.

I synthesized the list of words from the Spelling Bee.

I performed in the Spelling Bee with others in my class until there was a winner.

Little House Social Studies Curriculum Guide ©2005

Teacher Scoring Guide

Title: | **Lesson 28 - Spelling Bee**

[4] Exemplary	o Effective concluding of the history of the Literary including a Spelling Bee. o Clearly addresses the concept of the Spelling Bee using a word list. o Contains few errors synthesizing the words on the spelling word list. o Fluent performance in the Spelling Bee until there is a winner.

[3] Proficient	o Appropriately differentiates the history of the Literary including a Spelling Bee. o Focuses formulating the concept of the Spelling Bee using a word list. o Some errors synthesizing the words on the spelling word list. o Some weakness in performance in the Spelling Bee until there is a winner.

[2] Apprentice	o Unclear explaining the history of the Literary including a Spelling Bee o Weak progression distinguishing the concept of the Spelling Bee using a word list. o Many errors synthesizing the words on the spelling word list. o Inconsistent performance in the Spelling Bee until there is a winner.

[1] Novice	o Unclear naming the history of the Literary including a Spelling Bee. o Little or no recall of the concept of the Spelling Bee using a word list. o Lacks in synthesizing the words on the spelling word list. o Serious errors in performance in the Spelling Bee until there is a winner.

Lesson Plan

Title:	**Lesson 29 - Making a Hornbook**

Date:		Grade:	K-4

Suggested Season / Date: Spring / April, week 1

Time: 30 minutes (approx.)

Subject: Social Studies / History Activities

Learning Style / Different Multiple Intelligences: Tactile/Kinesthetic; Visual/Spatial Intelligence (activity could be used for all areas)

Example: hands on, doing, create and design a hornbook

Materials Needed:

1) *These Happy Golden Years*, pages 1-72
2) *Little House in the Classroom*, pages 101-108
3) *The World of Little House*, pages 98-105
4) *Across the Curriculum with Favorite Authors*, page 100
5) *Activities for Elementary School Social Studies*, page 2.12
6) *Little House Social Studies Curriculum Guide*, Activity, Performance Assessment Task, Student Scoring Guide, Teacher Scoring Guide: Lesson 29 - Making a Hornbook

Introduction:

1) Read from *These Happy Golden Years*.
2) Share information about school supplies when Laura taught.
3) The purpose is to learn about using a hornbook.

Major Instructional Sequence:

4) Provide pictures and information about school supplies. Explain concept of school supplies when Laura taught school.

Little House Social Studies Curriculum Guide ©2005

5) State definition concerning school supplies.
6) Provide examples of school supplies.
7) Check for understanding concerning school supplies used.

Concluding Sequence/Closure:

8) *Little House Social Studies Curriculum Guide*, Activity: Lesson 29 - Making a Hornbook

Evaluation:

9) *Little House Social Studies Curriculum Guide*, Performance Assessment Task, Student Scoring Guide, Teacher Scoring Guide: Lesson 29 - Making a Hornbook

Alignment to State Standards:

(compare to standards shown: Arkansas)

Strand 5:	Social Science Processes and Skills
Content Standard 1:	Students will demonstrate critical thinking skills through research, reading, writing, speaking, listening and problem-solving.

Learning Expectations

SSPS.1.1	Communicate knowledge and ideas in a variety of forms, such as reports, persuasive essays, journals, news articles, graphic displays, speeches, videos and stories.
SSPS.1.2	Recognize and discuss different perspectives in current and past issues.
SSPS.1.3	Interpret information from visual aids.

Activity

Title: **Lesson 29 - Making a Hornbook**

Sources:

1) *Activities for Elementary School Social Studies*, page 2.12

Materials Needed:

1) cardboard sheets measuring about 12" x 18" (per student)
2) marking pens in black or brown, beige construction paper
3) contact paper, glue
4) books with pictures of colonial classrooms and hornbooks

Objectives:

As a result of this activity, the student will:
o produce a representation of a hornbook
o create an original poem to go on the hornbook
o use the hornbook to simulate learning in a colonial schoolroom

Introduction:

1) Show pictures of colonial classrooms with hornbooks in use. Show close-up of a hornbook. Let students examine photographs closely.
2) Explain: since reading and writing material was scarce, schools used the thin outer cover of a cow's horn to cover and protect the paper, thus the name hornbook.
3) Tell students they will make a simulated hornbook out of cardboard.

Major Instructional Sequence:

4) Have students write their original poem on a sheet of tablet paper. Show students steps in constructing the hornbook:
    a. Cut cardboard into the shape of hornbook (rectangular with handle).
    b. Cut construction paper to fit top of cardboard hornbook.
    c. Neatly copy poem on to construction paper.
    d. Glue poem to cardboard hornbook and cover with contact paper.
5) Circulate and give assistance as students construct hornbooks.

Concluding Sequence/Closure:

6) Students show their hornbooks.
7) Students will share their writings with the class.

Little House Social Studies Curriculum Guide ©2005

Performance Assessment Task

Title: **Lesson 29 - Making a Hornbook**

Name:

Date:

Grade: K-4

Subject: Social Studies

Alignment to State Standards:
(minimum of three standards, input State standards below)

Code	Standard Description

Description of Performance Task:
(include time, student performance, assessment)

Time: 30 minutes (approx.)

Activity: Activity will correlate with reading *These Happy Golden Years*.

Task:
o Student will tell what a hornbook was in colonial days.
o Student will investigate books with pictures of colonial classrooms and hornbooks.
o Student will produce a representation of a hornbook using cardboard and art tools.
o Student will create a hornbook to simulate learning in colonial school room.
o Student will display their hornbook.

Student Scoring Guide: (attach a copy)

Teacher Scoring Guide: (attach a copy of scoring key)

Score (select one): [4] Exemplary [3] Proficient [2] Apprentice [1] Novice

Student Scoring Guide

Title: **Lesson 29 - Making a Hornbook**

Name:

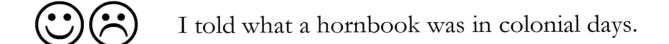 I told what a hornbook was in colonial days.

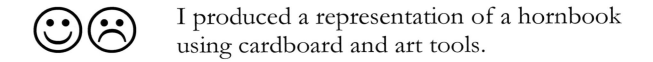 I investigated books with pictures of colonial classrooms and hornbooks.

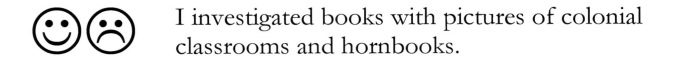 I produced a representation of a hornbook using cardboard and art tools.

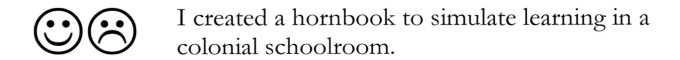 I created a hornbook to simulate learning in a colonial schoolroom.

I displayed my hornbook.

Little House Social Studies Curriculum Guide ©2005

Teacher Scoring Guide

Title: | **Lesson 29 - Making a Hornbook**

[4] Exemplary	o Effectively concludes what a hornbook was in colonial days.
	o Consistently appraising books with pictures of colonial classrooms and hornbooks.
	o Develops and illustrates a representation of a hornbook using cardboard and art tools.
	o Handles well displaying a hornbook.

[3] Proficient	o Clearly composes what a hornbook was in colonial days.
	o Some errors investigating books with pictures of colonial classrooms and hornbooks.
	o Appropriately produces a representation of a hornbook using cardboard and art tools.
	o Fairly strong display of a hornbook.

[2] Apprentice	o Inconsistent explaining of what a hornbook was in colonial days.
	o No particular order summarizing books with pictures of colonial classrooms and hornbooks.
	o Not clear representation of a hornbook using cardboard and art tools.
	o Many errors displaying a hornbook.

[1] Novice	o Little or no telling of what a hornbook was in colonial days.
	o Very little selecting of books with pictures of colonial classrooms and hornbooks.
	o Serious errors outlining a representation of a hornbook using cardboard and art tools.
	o Lacks labeling in display of a hornbook.

Lesson Plan

Title:	**Lesson 30 - Design a Handkerchief**

Date:		Grade:	K-4

Suggested Season / Date: | Spring / April, week 2

Time: | 30 minutes (approx.)

Subject: | Social Studies / Interdisciplinary Activities

Learning Style / Different Multiple Intelligences: | Tactile/Kinesthetic; Visual/Spatial Intelligence (activity could be used for all areas)

Example: | hands on, touching handkerchiefs and designing a handkerchief

Materials Needed:

1) *These Happy Golden Years*, pages 73-144
2) *The World of Little House*, pages 100-101
3) *My Little House Crafts Book*, pages 52-53 Adaptation
4) *Inside Laura's Little House*, pages 55-56
5) *Activities for Elementary School Social Studies*, page 7.7 Adaptation
6) *Little House Social Studies Curriculum Guide*, Activity, Performance Assessment Task, Student Scoring Guide, Teacher Scoring Guide: Lesson 30 - Design a Handkerchief

Introduction:

1) Read from *These Happy Golden Years*.
2) Share the history and usage for the handkerchief. Also, share other examples, such as bandanas.
3) The purpose is to understand and design a handkerchief.

Major Instructional Sequence:

4) Provide examples of handkerchiefs, napkins, bandanas and pillowcases.
5) State definitions concerning the household items.
6) Check for understanding for usage of household items.

Concluding Sequence/Closure:

7) *Little House Social Studies Curriculum Guide*, Activity: Lesson 30 - Design a Handkerchief

Evaluation:

8) *Little House Social Studies Curriculum Guide*, Performance Assessment Task, Student Scoring Guide, Teacher Scoring Guide: Lesson 30 - Design a Handkerchief

Alignment to State Standards:

(compare to standards shown: Arkansas)

Strand 1:	Time, Continuity and Change
Content Standard 2:	Students will demonstrate an understanding of how ideas, events and conditions bring about change.

Learning Expectations

TCC.2.3	Use personal experiences, biographies, autobiographies or historical fiction to explain how individuals are affected by, can cope with and can create change.
TCC.2.4	Explain how people, places, events, tools, institutions, attitudes, values and ideas are the result of what has gone before.
TCC.2.5	Use a variety of processes, such as thinking, reading, writing, listening and speaking, to demonstrate continuity and change.

Activity

Title: | **Lesson 30 - Design a Handkerchief**

Sources:

1) *Activities for Elementary School Social Studies*, page 7.7 Adaptation

Materials Needed:

1) construction paper in a variety of colors
2) crayons, pencils and marking pens
3) drawing paper
4) collection of handkerchiefs

Objectives:

As a result of this activity, the student will:
o understand history details and usage of the handkerchief
o express creativity in designing a handkerchief of bandana
o gain knowledge about usage of the handkerchief (as tissue)

Introduction:

1) Show students a variety of handkerchiefs, bandanas, napkins and pillowcases.
2) Tell students they are going to design a handkerchief or bandana.

Major Instructional Sequence:

3) Assemble materials and let students choose supplies.
4) Encourage students to be imaginative in designing a handkerchief or bandana.
5) Provide display of examples of handkerchiefs and bandanas.

Concluding Sequence/Closure:

6) Let students show and describe their individual handkerchief or bandana.
7) Display the handkerchiefs and bandanas.

Little House Social Studies Curriculum Guide ©2005

Performance Assessment Task

Title:	**Lesson 30 - Design a Handkerchief**		

Name:		Grade:	K-4
Date:		Subject:	Social Studies

Alignment to State Standards:
(minimum of three standards, input State standards below)

Code	Standard Description

Description of Performance Task:
(include time, student performance, assessment)

Time:	30 minutes (approx.)
Activity:	Activity will correlate with reading *These Happy Golden Years*.
Task:	o Student will identify and tell what a handkerchief is used for. o Student will observe a variety of beautiful handkerchiefs. o Student will design a representation of a handkerchief using drawing paper and art tools. o Student will be imaginative creating a handkerchief. o Student will share and display a handkerchief.

Student Scoring Guide: (attach a copy)

Teacher Scoring Guide: (attach a copy of scoring key)

Score (select one): [4] Exemplary [3] Proficient [2] Apprentice [1] Novice

Student Scoring Guide

Title: | **Lesson 30 - Design a Handkerchief**

Name:

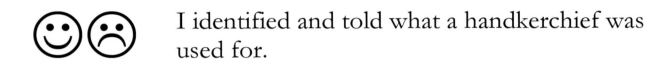 I identified and told what a handkerchief was used for.

I observed a numerous variety of beautiful colored and patterned handkerchiefs.

I designed a handkerchief using drawing paper and art tools.

I was imaginative in creating my handkerchief.

I shared about and displayed my beautiful handkerchief.

Teacher Scoring Guide

Title:	Lesson 30 - Design a Handkerchief

[4] Exemplary	o Effectively appraises a handkerchief and what it is used for. o Consistently validates a variety of beautiful handkerchiefs. o Contains few errors designing a representation of a handkerchief using drawing paper and art tools. o Handles well sharing and displaying a beautiful handkerchief with design.
[3] Proficient	o Reasonably differentiates a handkerchief and what it is used for. o Clearly relates a variety of beautiful handkerchiefs. o Appropriately imagines and creates a representation of a handkerchief using drawing paper and art tools. o Fairly strong sharing and displaying a beautiful handkerchief with design.
[2] Apprentice	o Inconsistent explaining a handkerchief and what it is used for. o Not focusing on a variety of beautiful handkerchiefs. o Many errors estimating a representation of a handkerchief using drawing paper and art tools. o No particular order generalizing and displaying a beautiful handkerchief with design.
[1] Novice	o Little or no identifying a handkerchief and what it is used for. o Very little naming of a variety of beautiful handkerchiefs. o Random labeling a representation of a handkerchief using drawing paper and art tools. o Serious errors describing and displaying a beautiful handkerchief with design.

Lesson Plan

Title:	**Lesson 31 - Writing a Letter**

Date:		Grade:	K-4

Suggested Season / Date:	Spring / April, week 3

Time:	30 minutes (approx.)

Subject:	Social Studies / Sociology Activities

Learning Style / Different Multiple Intelligences:	Tactile/Kinesthetic; Intrapersonal Intelligence (activity could be used for all areas)

Example:	hands on, doing, work alone and have their own space for writing

Materials Needed:

1) *These Happy Golden Years*, pages 145-216
2) *Mailing May*
3) Examples of written letters
4) *Activities for Elementary School Social Studies*, pages 4.10-4.11 Adaptation
5) *Little House Social Studies Curriculum Guide*, Activity, Performance Assessment Task, Student Scoring Guide, Teacher Scoring Guide: Lesson 31 - Writing a Letter

Introduction:

1) Read from *These Happy Golden Years*.
2) Share information about the history of the post office and writing letters.
3) The purpose is to compose a letter and mail it through the post office.

Major Instructional Sequence:

4) Provide information about writing various kinds of letters. Explain concept of writing letter and mailing it at the post office.

Little House Social Studies Curriculum Guide ©2005

5) Provide examples of cards and letters: thank you, invitation and friendly letter.
6) Check for understanding.

Concluding Sequence/Closure:

7) *Little House Social Studies Curriculum Guide*, Activity: Lesson 31 - Writing a Letter

Evaluation:

8) *Little House Social Studies Curriculum Guide*, Performance Assessment Task, Student Scoring Guide, Teacher Scoring Guide: Lesson 31 - Writing a Letter

Alignment to State Standards:

(compare to standards shown: Arkansas)

Strand 2:	People, Places and Environments
Content Standard 1:	Students will demonstrate an understanding that people, cultures and systems are connected and that commonalities and diversities exist among them.

Learning Expectations

PPE.1.2	Compare and contrast similarities and differences in cultures through a variety of experiences, such as reading, writing, drawing, role-playing, dance, music and simulation.
PPE.1.5	Analyze the effects of interactions between people and their environment.
PPE.1.7	Use a variety of processes, such as thinking, listening, reading, writing and speaking, to analyze interdependence.

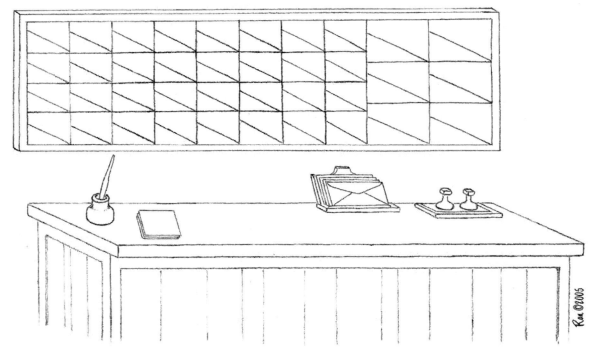

Activity

Title: | **Lesson 31 - Writing a Letter**

Sources:

1) *Activities for Elementary School Social Studies*, pages 4.10-4.11 Adaptation

Materials Needed:

1) *Mailing May*
2) reference materials explaining writing letters
3) examples of various kinds of writing (such as cards, invitations and friendly letters)
4) assortment of stationery writing paper and pencils

Objectives:

As a result of this activity, the student will:
o produce a written letter ready for mailing
o research about the history of the post office and letter writing
o increase knowledge of writing

Introduction:

1) Talk about letters and how nice it would be to receive a letter.
2) Let students examine examples of letters, cards and invitations.
3) Tell students they will write a letter and mail it.

Major Instructional Sequence:

4) Tell students they will select stationery and pencils for writing.
5) Let students begin constructing a letter.
6) Circulate and check for understanding, giving assistance.

Concluding Sequence/Closure:

7) Let student read their letter to the class.
8) Place letter in envelope ready to mail.

Little House Social Studies Curriculum Guide ©2005

Performance Assessment Task

Title:	**Lesson 31 - Writing a Letter**		
Name:		Grade:	K-4
Date:		Subject:	Social Studies

Alignment to State Standards:
(minimum of three standards, input State standards below)

Code	Standard Description

Description of Performance Task:
(include time, student performance, assessment)

Time:	30 minutes (approx.)
Activity:	Activity will correlate with reading *These Happy Golden Years*.
Task:	o Student will identify why you would write a letter and to whom. o Student will investigate various kinds of writing: cards, invitations and friendly letter. o Student will understand why you would mail the letter at the post office. o Student will demonstrate letter writing by constructing a friendly letter using stationery and a pencil. o Student will perform writing and mailing a letter.

Student Scoring Guide: | (attach a copy)

Teacher Scoring Guide: | (attach a copy of scoring key)
Score (select one): | [4] Exemplary [3] Proficient [2] Apprentice [1] Novice

Student Scoring Guide

Title: **Lesson 31 - Writing a Letter**

Name:

 I identified why someone would write a letter and to whom.

 I investigated various kinds of writing: cards, invitations and friendly letter. I understood why you would mail it at the post office.

 I demonstrated letter writing by constructing a friendly letter using stationery and a pencil.

 I communicated by putting the letter in the mail.

 I performed the process of writing and mailing a letter.

Little House Social Studies Curriculum Guide ©2005

Teacher Scoring Guide

Title: | **Lesson 31 - Writing a Letter**

[4] Exemplary	o Effectively concludes to whom a letter was written and why.
	o Clearly addresses comparing various kinds of writing such as friendly letters, cards and invitations.
	o Fluently formulates constructing a friendly letter using stationery and a pencil.
	o Consistently performs the process of writing and mailing a letter.

[3] Proficient	o Reasonably deduces to whom a letter was written and why.
	o Focuses on relating various kinds of writing such as friendly letters, cards and invitations.
	o Appropriately demonstrates a friendly letter using stationery and a pencil.
	o Fairly strong illustration of the process of writing and mailing a letter.

[2] Apprentice	o Inconsistent distinguishes to whom a letter was written and why.
	o Not clear discriminating various kinds of writing such as friendly letters, cards and invitations.
	o Not much information extending a friendly letter using stationery and a pencil.
	o Many errors summarizing the process of writing and mailing a letter.

[1] Novice	o Little or no identifying to whom a letter was written and why.
	o Very little selection of various kinds of writing as friendly letters, cards and invitations.
	o Serious errors stating a friendly letter using stationery and a pencil.
	o Unclear defining the process of writing and mailing a letter.

Lesson Plan

Title:	**Lesson 32 - *Little House* Dinner**

Date:		Grade:	K-4

Suggested Season / Date:	Spring / April, week 4

Time:	30 minutes (approx. plus shopping, preparation and clean up)

Subject:	Social Studies / Economic Activities

Learning Style / Different Multiple Intelligences:	Tactile/Kinesthetic; Naturalistic Intelligence (activity could be used for all areas)

Example:	hands on, eating and sampling garden vegetables and other foods eaten in colonial days

Materials Needed:

1) *These Happy Golden Years*, pages 217-289
2) *Little House Cookbook* (parent choices)
3) *The World of Little House*, page 131
4) *Little House in the Classroom*, page 25
5) *Across the Curriculum with Favorite Authors*, pages 21, 58, 82, 84
6) *Activities for Elementary School Social Studies*, pages 5.15-5.16 Adaptation
7) *Little House Social Studies Curriculum Guide*, Activity, Performance Assessment Task, Student Scoring Guide, Teacher Scoring Guide: Lesson 32 - *Little House* Dinner

Introduction:

1) Read from *These Happy Golden Years*.
2) Share about meals for every day.

Major Instructional Sequence:

3) Provide information about what Laura's family ate on a regular basis.

4) Explain concepts on how they grew food and what food was needed from the general store.

5) Assign a food to each student for shopping, preparing and bringing the *Little House* Dinner. Ask parents for help via letter: assist in preparation, set up and clean up.

6) Ask questions for understanding.

Concluding Sequence/Closure:

7) *Little House Social Studies Curriculum Guide*, Activity: Lesson 32 - *Little House* Dinner

Evaluation:

8) *Little House Social Studies Curriculum Guide*, Performance Assessment Task, Student Scoring Guide, Teacher Scoring Guide: Lesson 32 - *Little House* Dinner

Alignment to State Standards:

(compare to standards shown: Arkansas)

Strand 2:	People, Places and Environments
Content Standard 1:	Students will demonstrate an understanding that people, cultures and systems are connected and that commonalities and diversities exist among them.

Learning Expectations

PPE.1.1	Investigate how members of a family, school, community, state, nation and culture depend on each other.
PPE.1.2	Compare and contrast similarities and differences in cultures through a variety of experiences, such as reading, writing, drawing, role-playing, dance, music and simulation.
PPE.1.7	Use a variety of processes, such as thinking, listening, reading, writing and speaking, to analyze interdependence.

Activity

Title:	**Lesson 32 - *Little House* Dinner**

Sources:

1) *Activities for Elementary School Social Studies*, pages 5.15-5.16 Adaptation

Materials Needed:

1) food brought by each student that would have been eaten in the colonial days
2) napkins, paper goods
3) parent participation: preparing, serving and clean up of dinner

Objectives:

As a result of this activity, the student will:
o understand what was eaten on a daily basis
o relay different ways of shopping for foods then (general store) and now
o work cooperatively to put together a *Little House* Dinner

Introduction:

1) Divide dinner by each student bringing a food (or paper goods) to contribute.
2) List items of food on chalkboard (send in parent letter – request) that student offers to bring.

Major Instructional Sequence:

3) Parents will participate by shopping, preparing and bringing foods for *Little House* dinner.
4) Students will eat the foods that Laura would have eaten in colonial days.
5) Circulate and talk about how the foods are different from what we eat today.

Concluding Sequence/Closure:

6) Determine how foods were obtained and prepared differently then (gardens vs. shopping at the general store).
7) Give opportunity to share about the foods they ate.

Performance Assessment Task

Title:	**Lesson 32 - *Little House* Dinner**

Name:		Grade:	K-4
Date:		Subject:	Social Studies

Alignment to State Standards:
(minimum of three standards, input State standards below)

Code	Standard Description

Description of Performance Task:
(include time, student performance, assessment)

Time:	30 minutes (approx.)
Activity:	Activity will correlate with reading *These Happy Golden Years*.
Task:	o Student will describe foods people ate in colonial days.

o Student will investigate, discuss and plan at home what they might bring for the *Little House* dinner.
o Student will demonstrate by bringing one of the foods eaten in colonial days to share for the dinner.
o Student will help the class create the dinner with the help of parents.
o Student will share in eating the foods eaten in colonial days.

Student Scoring Guide:	(attach a copy)

Teacher Scoring Guide:	(attach a copy of scoring key)
Score (select one):	[4] Exemplary [3] Proficient [2] Apprentice [1] Novice

Student Scoring Guide

Title: **Lesson 32 - *Little House* Dinner**

Name:

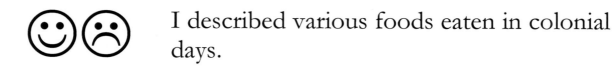 I described various foods eaten in colonial days.

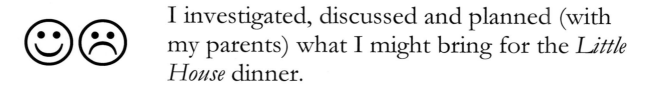 I investigated, discussed and planned (with my parents) what I might bring for the *Little House* dinner.

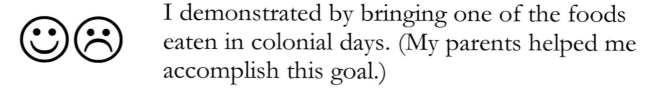 I demonstrated by bringing one of the foods eaten in colonial days. (My parents helped me accomplish this goal.)

I helped the class create the *Little House* dinner (with the help of my parents).

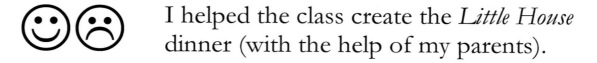 I shared about eating of the *Little House* dinner.

Little House Social Studies Curriculum Guide ©2005

Teacher Scoring Guide

Title: | **Lesson 32 - *Little House* Dinner**

---

[4] Exemplary
- Clearly addresses and validates food eaten in colonial days.
- Handles well concluding what food might be prepared for the *Little House* dinner.
- Effectively compiles and brings food to share in creating the *Little House* dinner.
- Fluently shares about the foods eaten and enjoyed at the *Little House* dinner.

---

[3] Proficient
- Appropriately categorizes food eaten in colonial days.
- Focuses on deducing what food might be prepared for the *Little House* dinner.
- Apparently differentiates and brings food to share in illustrating the *Little House* dinner.
- Ideas progress about the foods eaten and enjoyed at the *Little House* dinner.

---

[2] Apprentice
- Basically explains food eaten in colonial days.
- Not much information devising what food might be prepared for the *Little House* dinner.
- Contains some estimation and brings food to share in discriminating the *Little House* dinner.
- Not elaborately summarizes about the foods eaten and enjoyed at the *Little House* dinner.

---

[1] Novice
- Unclearly recalls food eaten in colonial days.
- Very little identifying what food might be prepared for the *Little House* dinner.
- Little or no describing and brings food to share in the *Little House* dinner.
- Random stating about the foods eaten and enjoyed at the *Little House* dinner.

Lesson Plan

Title: **Lesson 33 - Developing a Timeline**

Date: **Grade:** K-4

Suggested Season / Date: Spring / May, week 1

Time: 30 minutes (approx.)

Subject: Social Studies / History Activities

Learning Style / Different Multiple Intelligences: Visual; Interpersonal Intelligence (activity could be used for all areas)

Example: seeing visuals, magazines, newspapers, articles, cartoons, drawings, photographs; organize/cooperate to form a timeline

Materials Needed:

1) *The First Four Years*, pages 1-34
2) *Little House in the Classroom*, pages 3-16
3) *The World of Little House*, pages 111-121
4) *Across the Curriculum with Favorite Authors*, pages 3-13
5) *Activities for Elementary School Social Studies*, pages 2.16-2.17 Adaptation
6) *Little House Social Studies Curriculum Guide*, Activity, Performance Assessment Task, Student Scoring Guide, Teacher Scoring Guide: Lesson 33 - Developing a Timeline

Introduction:

1) Read from *The First Four Years*.
2) Share information about Laura's timeline from sources.
3) The purpose is to learn about the timeline of Laura's life.

Major Instructional Sequence:

4) Provide information and pictures about Laura's life.
5) Explain concept of timeline. State definitions used in timeline.
6) Modeling: provide timeline of the teacher's life.
7) Ask questions and check for understanding of timeline.

Concluding Sequence/Closure:

8) *Little House Social Studies Curriculum Guide*, Activity: Lesson 33 - Developing a Timeline

Evaluation:

9) *Little House Social Studies Curriculum Guide*, Performance Assessment Task, Student Scoring Guide, Teacher Scoring Guide: Lesson 33 - Developing a Timeline

Alignment to State Standards:

(compare to standards shown: Arkansas)

Strand 1:	Time, Continuity and Change
Content Standard 2:	Students will demonstrate an understanding of how ideas, events and conditions bring about change.

Learning Expectations

TCC.2.1	Discuss and record changes in one's self, community, state and nation.
TCC.2.3	Use personal experiences, biographies, autobiographies or historical fiction to explain how individuals are affected by, can cope with, creates change.
TCC.2.4	Explain how people, places, events, tools, institutions, attitudes, values and ideas are the result of what has gone before.

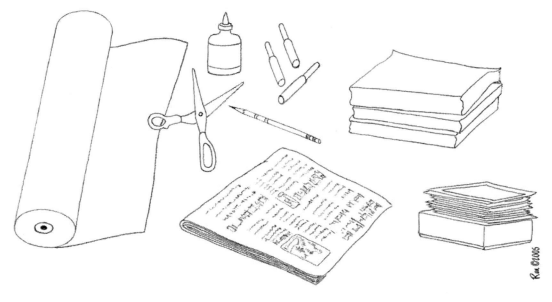

Activity

Title: **Lesson 33 - Developing a Timeline**

Sources:

1) *Activities for Elementary School Social Studies*, pages 2.16-2.17 Adaptation

Materials Needed:

1) long strip of butcher paper (15-20 feet long)
2) glue, scissors, tape, marking pens
3) old magazines, newspapers, catalogs dating back to time of students' birthdays
4) photographs of students (and families) at various stages, from baby to present day
5) model: timeline of teacher's lifetime (prepared in advance)

Objectives:

As a result of this activity, the student will:
o interpret and display historical information in graphic form
o work cooperatively with other students to develop a large timeline depicting events in all their lifetimes

Introduction:

1) Demonstrate timeline of teacher's life, explaining that it begins when the teacher was born up to the present time. Let students examine the timeline closely, looking at the photos, etc., to see that they correlate with different dates/times.

Major Instructional Sequence:

2) By a show of hands, determine which student has the earliest (oldest) birthday. Let student mark birthday (day, month, year) at the beginning of the timeline.
3) Continue with the next oldest student, until all students have recorded their birth dates on the timeline, spacing each about five inches apart.
4) Have students place subsequent years on the timeline about eighteen inches apart.
5) Tape students' photos under appropriate time periods (baby photo: birth date).
6) Students search through the old magazines, etc. to find significant headlines, photos, etc. to be cut out and glued on the timeline under the appropriate years.

Concluding Sequence/Closure:

7) Each student goes to the timeline and explains their pictures and contributions.
8) Display the timeline in the classroom.

Little House Social Studies Curriculum Guide ©2005

Performance Assessment Task

Title:	**Lesson 33 - Developing a Timeline**

Name:		Grade:	K-4
Date:		Subject:	Social Studies

Alignment to State Standards:
(minimum of three standards, input State standards below)

Code	Standard Description

Description of Performance Task:
(include time, student performance, assessment)

Time:	30 minutes (approx.)
Activity:	Activity will correlate with reading *The First Four Years*.
Task:	o Student will describe a timeline concept looking at pictures of Laura. o Student will observe and discuss a model timeline of the teacher. o Student will demonstrate a timeline using pictures, old magazines, catalogs and butcher paper. o Student will tape their photos beneath their birth dates. o Student will differentiate time using their pictures and contributions. o Student will display the timeline in the classroom.

Student Scoring Guide: | (attach a copy)

Teacher Scoring Guide: | (attach a copy of scoring key)

Score (select one): | [4] Exemplary [3] Proficient [2] Apprentice [1] Novice

Student Scoring Guide

Title: **Lesson 33 - Developing a Timeline**

Name:

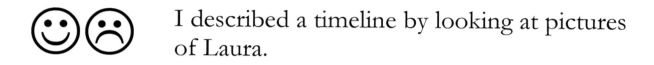 I described a timeline by looking at pictures of Laura.

☺☹ I observed and discussed a model timeline of my teacher.

☺☹ I demonstrated a timeline using butcher paper, old magazines, catalogs and old photos depicting events since my birth.

☺☹ I differentiated between time using dates and pictures on the butcher paper timeline.

☺☹ I displayed the timeline in the classroom.

Little House Social Studies Curriculum Guide ©2005

Teacher Scoring Guide

Title:	**Lesson 33 - Developing a Timeline**

---

[4] Exemplary

o Effectively contrasts a timeline looking at pictures of Laura.
o Clearly addresses and categorizes a model timeline observing the teacher's timeline.
o Contains few errors devising a timeline using butcher paper, old photos, magazines and catalogs.
o Handles well displaying a timeline in the classroom.

---

[3] Proficient

o Reasonably relates to a timeline looking at pictures of Laura.
o Appropriately discusses a model timeline observing the teacher's timeline.
o Fairly strong in developing a timeline using butcher paper, old photos, magazines and catalogs.
o Some weakness displaying a timeline in the classroom.

---

[2] Apprentice

o Inconsistent explaining of timeline looking at pictures of Laura.
o Not too clear relating to a model timeline observing the teacher's timeline.
o Not much information converting a timeline using butcher paper, old photos, magazines and catalogs.
o Many errors displaying a timeline in the classroom.

---

[1] Novice

o Little or no naming of timeline looking at pictures of Laura.
o Very little observations of a model timeline observing the teacher's timeline.
o Lacks listing on a timeline using butcher paper, old photos, magazines and catalogs.
o Random displaying of a timeline in the classroom.

Lesson Plan

Title:	**Lesson 34 - Picture Yourself There**
Date:	Grade: K-4
Suggested Season / Date:	Spring / May, week 2
Time:	30 minutes (approx.)
Subject:	Social Studies / History Activities
Learning Style / Different Multiple Intelligences:	Tactile/Kinesthetic; Visual/Spatial Intelligences (activity could be used for all areas)
Example:	hands on, touching, doing and creating a corncob doll

Materials Needed:

1) *The First Four Years*, pages 35-67
2) *Little House in the Classroom*, pages 19-20
3) *The World of Little House*, pages vii-11
4) *Activities for Elementary School Social Studies*, pages 4.27-4.28
5) *Little House Social Studies Curriculum Guide*, Activity, Performance Assessment Task, Student Scoring Guide, Teacher Scoring Guide: Lesson 34 - Picture Yourself There

Introduction:

1) Read from *The First Four Years*.
2) Share about work and fun activities of Laura and her family.
3) The purpose is to learn what Laura's family did for work and fun.

Major Instructional Sequence:

4) Provide information about what Laura's family did for work and fun. Explain concepts introduced about hunting, fishing and trapping. Explain concepts about their fun activities as making a corncob doll. State needed definitions.

Little House Social Studies Curriculum Guide ©2005

5) Give examples and show pictures from other sources.
6) Ask questions for understanding.

Concluding Sequence/Closure:

7) *Little House Social Studies Curriculum Guide*, Activity: Lesson 34 - Picture Yourself There

Evaluation:

8) *Little House Social Studies Curriculum Guide*, Performance Assessment Task, Student Scoring Guide, Teacher Scoring Guide: Lesson 34 - Picture Yourself There

Alignment to State Standards:

(compare to standards shown: Arkansas)

Strand 3:	Production, Distribution and Consumption
Content Standard 1:	Students will demonstrate an understanding that different economic systems and limited resources influence cooperation and conflict in decision making.

Learning Expectations

PDC.1.4	Use a variety of thinking processes, such as reading, writing, speaking, listening, estimating, predicting, to analyze and apply concepts of scarcity and choice.
PDC.1.9	Explore the kinds of work that people do and how that work benefits their family and community.
PDC.1.10	Identify and define ways of spending and saving money.

Activity

Title: **Lesson 34 - Picture Yourself There**

Sources:

1) *Activities for Elementary School Social Studies*, pages 4.27-4.28

Materials Needed:

1) construction paper in assorted colors
2) corncobs
3) scrap fabric
4) magazines

Objectives:

As a result of this activity, the student will:

o draw picture of self in imagined *Little House* setting
o create a corncob doll using corncob and scrap of fabric
o cut out pictures of hunting, fishing, trapping

Introduction:

1) Discuss Laura's family in rural setting.
2) Discuss different activities which might occur in *Little House* setting:
   a. Pa hunting, fishing and trapping / playing fiddle
   b. Laura making and playing with her corncob doll
3) Tell students they will make their own corncob doll.

Major Instructional Sequence:

4) Students draw and color a picture of themselves in the rural setting.
5) Students will make their own corncob doll.
6) Students will cut out pictures of hunting, fishing, trapping.
7) Students will listen to tape of Pa playing fiddle.

Concluding Sequence/Closure:

8) Let each student show and tell about picture of self in an imagined setting.
9) Display pictures of work: hunt, fish and trap.
10) Let students play with doll while listening to Pa play fiddle.

Performance Assessment Task

Title:	**Lesson 34 - Picture Yourself There**

Name:		Grade:	K-4
Date:		Subject:	Social Studies

Alignment to State Standards:
(minimum of three standards, input State standards below)

Code	Standard Description

Description of Performance Task:
(include time, student performance, assessment)

Time:	30 minutes (approx.)
Activity:	Activity will correlate with reading *The First Four Years*.
Task:	o Student will identify what Laura and her family did for work and play. o Student will cut out pictures of hunting, fishing and trapping out of magazines. o Student will make corncob doll o Student will draw pictures of self in an imagined rural setting. o Student will show class their corncob doll. o Student will display pictures of work: hunting, fishing and trapping.

Student Scoring Guide:	(attach a copy)

Teacher Scoring Guide:	(attach a copy of scoring key)
Score (select one):	[4] Exemplary [3] Proficient [2] Apprentice [1] Novice

Student Scoring Guide

Title: **Lesson 34 - Picture Yourself There**

Name:

 I identified what Laura's family did for work (hunt, fish, trap) and fun (play the fiddle, make a corncob doll).

 I discussed what Laura and her family did for work and play.

 I used a variety of pictures, magazines, construction paper to show work. I used corncob and fabric to make a corncob doll.

 I differentiated between what Laura and her family did for work and play.

 I displayed work (pictures of hunt, fish and trap) and play (made a corncob doll).

Teacher Scoring Guide

Title: | **Lesson 34 - Picture Yourself There**

[4] Exemplary	o Effectively compares and contrasts what Laura's family did for work (hunt, fish and trap) and for play (play the fiddle, make a corncob doll).
	o Clearly addresses how to make a corncob doll with a corncob and fabric.
	o Handles well interpreting pictures, magazines, construction paper to show hunting, fishing, trapping.
	o Consistent display of work and play.

[3] Proficient	o Reasonably summarizes what Laura's family did for work (hunt, fish and trap) and for play (play the fiddle, make a corncob doll).
	o Focuses on illustrating how to make a corncob doll with a corncob and fabric
	o Appropriately uses pictures, magazines, construction paper to show hunting, fishing, trapping
	o Fairly strong display of work and play.

[2] Apprentice	o Inconsistently generalizes what Laura's family did for work (hunt, fish and trap) and for play (play the fiddle, make a corncob doll).
	o Many errors distinguishing how to make a corncob doll with a corncob and fabric
	o Significant weakness inferring pictures, magazines, construction paper to show hunting, fishing, trapping
	o No particular order to display of work and play.

[1] Novice	o Little or no naming of what Laura's family did for work (hunt, fish and trap) and for play (play the fiddle, make a corncob doll).
	o Unclear identifying how to make a corncob doll with a corncob and fabric.
	o Random selecting pictures, magazines, construction paper to show hunting, fishing, trapping
	o Sparse display of work and play.

Lesson Plan

Title:	**Lesson 35 - Observe Change**

Date:		Grade:	K-4

Suggested Season / Date:	Spring / May, week 3

Time:	30 minutes (approx.)

Subject:	Social Studies / Sociology Activities

Learning Style / Different Multiple Intelligences:	Visual; Verbal/Linguistic Intelligence (activity could be used for all areas)

Example:	seeing old photographs, artifacts, examine and tell family stories

Materials Needed:

1) *The First Four Years*, pages 68-101
2) *Little House in the Classroom*, pages 3, 4, 17-24
3) *The World of Little House*, pages vii, 1-20
4) *Activities for Elementary School Social Studies*, pages 4.4-4.5
5) *Little House Social Studies Curriculum Guide*, Activity, Performance Assessment Task, Student Scoring Guide, Teacher Scoring Guide: Lesson 35 - Observe Change

Introduction:

1) Read from *The First Four Years*.
2) Share background information on Laura and her family.
3) The purpose is to observe change of Laura and her family.

Major Instructional Sequence:

4) Provide information about Laura and her family. Explain concepts and state definitions needed.
5) Give examples from other sources.

Little House Social Studies Curriculum Guide ©2005

6) Ask questions for understanding.

Concluding Sequence/Closure:

7) *Little House Social Studies Curriculum Guide*, Activity: Lesson 35 - Observe Change

Evaluation:

8) *Little House Social Studies Curriculum Guide*, Performance Assessment Task, Student Scoring Guide, Teacher Scoring Guide: Lesson 35 - Observe Change

Alignment to State Standards:

(compare to standards shown: Arkansas)

Strand 1:	Time, Continuity and Change
Content Standard 1:	Students will demonstrate an understanding of the chronology, concepts of history, identify and explain historical relationships.

Learning Expectations

TCC.1.1	Examine and analyze stories of important Americans and their contributions to our society.
TCC.1.2	Explain how individuals, events and ideas influence the history of one's self, family, community, state and nation.
TCC.1.6	Use vocabulary related to time and chronology.

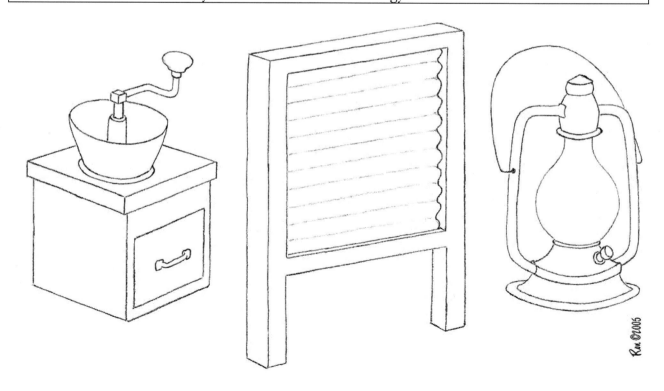

Activity

Title: | **Lesson 35 - Observe Change**

Sources:

1) *Activities for Elementary School Social Studies*, pages 4.4-4.5

Materials Needed:

1) journal book
2) family artifacts (send suggestion list to parents)
3) old family photographs
4) newsletter to parents: prior to activity, ask parents to send stories

Objectives:

As a result of this activity, the student will:
o describe family artifacts
o examine old photographs showing family
o write in journal books about artifacts and old photographs

Introduction:

1) Call attention to family artifacts.
2) Discuss family pictures.

Major Instructional Sequence:

3) Show and tell about old photographs and artifacts (items such as wooden eggs, ancient waffle iron, handcrafted salt and pepper shakers, newspapers, cooking utensils, old photographs).
4) Share the family story along with the artifact they bring.

Concluding Sequence/Closure:

5) Student will write in journal books about artifacts and old photographs.
6) Student will share journal writings with class.
7) Student will make a display of old photographs and artifacts.

Performance Assessment Task

Title:	**Lesson 35 - Observe Change**

Name:		Grade:	K-4
Date:		Subject:	Social Studies

Alignment to State Standards:
(minimum of three standards, input State standards below)

Code	Standard Description

Description of Performance Task:
(include time, student performance, assessment)

Time:	30 minutes (approx.)
Activity:	Activity will correlate with reading *The First Four Years*.
Task:	o Student will describe change in Laura's family over time.
	o Student will bring old family photographs, artifacts and family stories.
	o Student will explain about old photographs, artifacts and any family stories.
	o Student will examine old photographs and artifacts.
	o Student will write about old photographs and artifacts.
	o Student will display old family photographs and artifacts.

Student Scoring Guide: | (attach a copy)

Teacher Scoring Guide: | (attach a copy of scoring key)

Score (select one): | [4] Exemplary [3] Proficient [2] Apprentice [1] Novice

Student Scoring Guide

Title: **Lesson 35 - Observe Change**

Name:

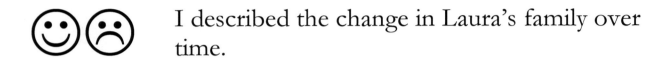 I described the change in Laura's family over time.

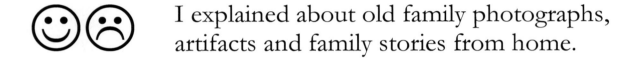 I explained about old family photographs, artifacts and family stories from home.

I examined old family photographs and artifacts.

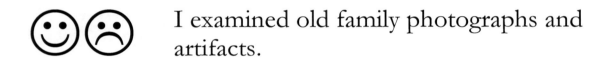 I analyzed and wrote about old family photographs, artifacts and family stories from home.

I displayed old family photographs and artifacts.

Little House Social Studies Curriculum Guide ©2005

Teacher Scoring Guide

Title: | **Lesson 35 - Observe Change**

[4] Exemplary	o Effective comparing of change in Laura's family over time.
	o Clearly addresses concluding about old family photographs, artifacts and family stories from home.
	o Contains few errors examining old family photographs, artifacts and family stories from home.
	o Fluently composes and displays old family photographs and artifacts from home.

[3] Proficient	o Apparently relates to change in Laura's family over time.
	o Appropriately deduces about old family photographs, artifacts and family stories from home.
	o Some errors differentiating about old family photos, artifacts and family stories from home.
	o Reasonably outlines and displays old family photographs and artifacts from home.

[2] Apprentice	o Inconsistent discussing about change in Laura's family over time.
	o Many errors explaining about old family photographs, artifacts and family stories from home.
	o No particular order to distinguishing old family photographs, artifacts and family stories from home.
	o Repetitively describes and displays old family photographs and artifacts from home.

[1] Novice	o Lacks evidence of naming change in Laura's family over time.
	o Little or no stating of old family photographs, artifacts and family stories from home.
	o Serious errors recalling about old family photographs, artifacts and stories from home.
	o Little or no labeling or display of old family photographs and artifacts from home.

Lesson Plan

Title:	**Lesson 36 - Fiddle Music**

Date:		Grade:	K-4

Suggested Season / Date: Spring / May, week 4

Time: 30 minutes (approx.)

Subject: Social Studies / Anthropology Activities

Learning Style / Different Multiple Intelligences: Auditory; Musical Rhythmic Intelligence (activity could be used for all areas)

Example: listening, ability to appreciate fiddle music, sounds, rhythms and patterns

Materials Needed:

1) *The First Four Years*, pages 102-134
2) *World of Little House*, pages 16, 22, 78, 128
3) *Little House in the Classroom*, page 66
4) *Across the Curriculum with Favorite Authors*, page 107
5) *My Little House Songbook and Tape*, pages 8, 12, 14, 22
6) Laura Ingalls Wilder Speaks (cassette tape)
7) *Activities for Elementary School Social Studies*, pages 5.11-5.12 Adaptation
8) *Little House Social Studies Curriculum Guide*, Activity, Performance Assessment Task, Student Scoring Guide, Teacher Scoring Guide: Lesson 36 - Fiddle Music

Introduction:

1) Read from *The First Four Years*.
2) Share background information about the fiddle/violin.
3) The purpose is to listen to, learn about and appreciate fiddle music.

Little House Social Studies Curriculum Guide ©2005

Major Instructional Sequence:

4) Provide fiddle music, fiddle and fiddle player (possibly).
5) Listen to fiddle music. Share information about the fiddle.
6) Ask questions for understanding.

Concluding Sequence/Closure:

7) *Little House Social Studies Curriculum Guide*, Activity: Lesson 36 - Fiddle Music

Evaluation:

8) *Little House Social Studies Curriculum Guide*, Performance Assessment Task, Student Scoring Guide, Teacher Scoring Guide: Lesson 36 - Fiddle Music

Alignment to State Standards:

(compare to standards shown: Arkansas)

Strand 1:	Time, Continuity and Change
Content Standard 2:	Students will demonstrate an understanding of how ideas, events and conditions bring about change.

Learning Expectations

TCC.2.3	Use personal experiences, biographies, autobiographies or historical fiction to explain how individuals are affected by, can cope with and can create change.
TCC.2.4	Explain how people, places, events, tools, institutions, attitudes, values and ideas are the result of what has bone before.
TCC.2.5	Use a variety of processes, such as thinking, reading, writing, listening and speaking, to demonstrate continuity and change.

Title: | **Lesson 36 - Fiddle Music** |

Sources:

1) *Activities for Elementary School Social Studies*, pages 5.11-5.12 Adaptation

Materials Needed:

1) books about the fiddle
2) fiddle, fiddle music
3) fiddle player (possibly)

Objectives:

As a result of this activity, the student will:
o   distinguish fiddle music
o   research about the fiddle
o   appreciate listening to fiddle music

Introduction:

1) Introduce the fiddle and information about the fiddle as the history and making of the fiddle.
2) Brainstorm about comparing the fiddle to other instruments.

Major Instructional Sequence:

3) Have students listen to taped fiddle music.
4) Have students listen to fiddle player (if one is available).
5) Circulate and give assist with understanding as needed.

Concluding Sequence/Closure:

6) Let students share about the fiddle music.
7) May journal about fiddle music.

Performance Assessment Task

Title:	**Lesson 36 - Fiddle Music**		

Name:		Grade:	K-4
Date:		Subject:	Social Studies

Alignment to State Standards:
(minimum of three standards, input State standards below)

Code	Standard Description

Description of Performance Task:
(include time, student performance, assessment)

Time:	30 minutes (approx.)
Activity:	Activity will correlate with reading *The First Four Years*.
Task:	o Student will identify and describe the fiddle and fiddle music. o Student will use a variety of resources to learn about the fiddle and fiddle music. o Student will listen to taped or live fiddle and fiddle music. o Student will share about the fiddle and fiddle music. o Student will write about the seeing the fiddle and listening to fiddle music.

Student Scoring Guide: | (attach a copy)

Teacher Scoring Guide: | (attach a copy of scoring key)

Score (select one): | [4] Exemplary [3] Proficient [2] Apprentice [1] Novice

Student Scoring Guide

Title: **Lesson 36 - Fiddle Music**

Name:

☺☹ I identified the fiddle and fiddle music.

☺☹ I examined resources to learn about the fiddle and fiddle music.

☺☹ I related listening to the fiddle and fiddle music.

☺☹ I shared about the fiddle and fiddle music.

☺☹ I wrote about seeing the fiddle and hearing fiddle music.

Little House Social Studies Curriculum Guide ©2005

Teacher Scoring Guide

Title: | **Lesson 36 - Fiddle Music**

---

[4] Exemplary
- o Effectively interprets about the fiddle and fiddle music.
- o Clearly addresses using a variety of resources to learn more about the fiddle and fiddle music.
- o Genuinely appraises taped or live fiddle music.
- o Fluently shares and writes about the fiddle and fiddle music.

---

[3] Proficient
- o Reasonably deduces about the fiddle and fiddle music.
- o Appropriately demonstrates using a variety of resources to learn more about the fiddle and fiddle music.
- o Focuses on relating to taped or live fiddle music.
- o Clearly differentiates and writes about the fiddle and fiddle music.

---

[2] Apprentice
- o Inconsistent explaining about the fiddle and fiddle music.
- o Many errors in discrimination of using a variety of resources to learn more about the fiddle and fiddle music.
- o Not focused on distinguishing taped or live fiddle music.
- o Not elaborate explaining or writing about the fiddle and fiddle music.

---

[1] Novice
- o Little or no recall about the fiddle and fiddle music.
- o Unclear telling about using a variety of resources to learn more about the fiddle and fiddle music.
- o Lacks identifying taped or live fiddle music.
- o Random selecting or writing about the fiddle and fiddle music.

Activity Worksheets

Name

Name

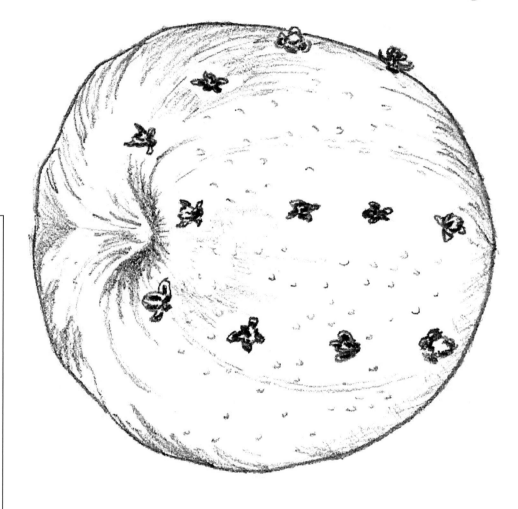

Ron @2005

Name

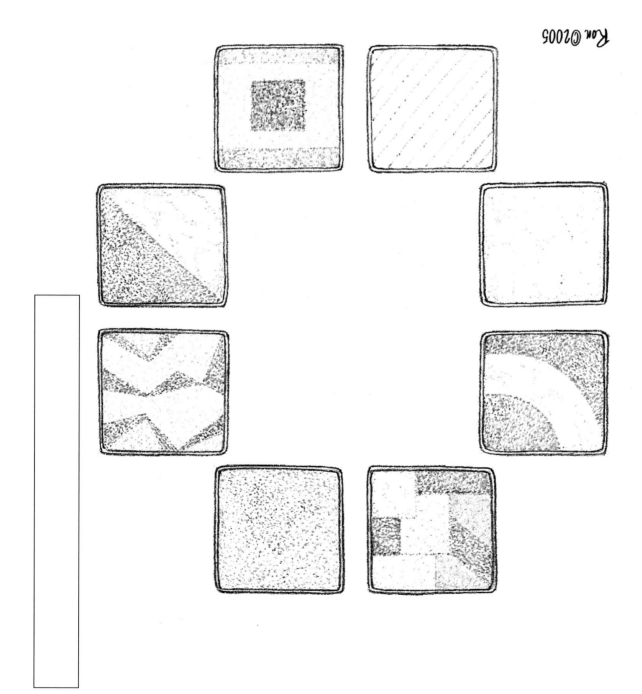

Ron @2005

Ron @2005

Name

Name

Ron @2005

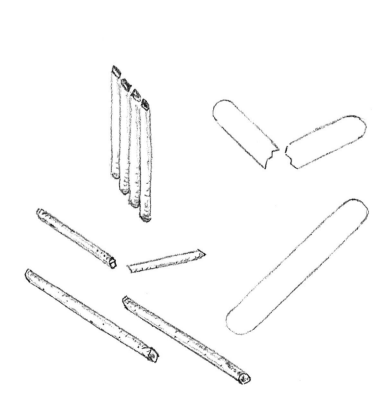

Name

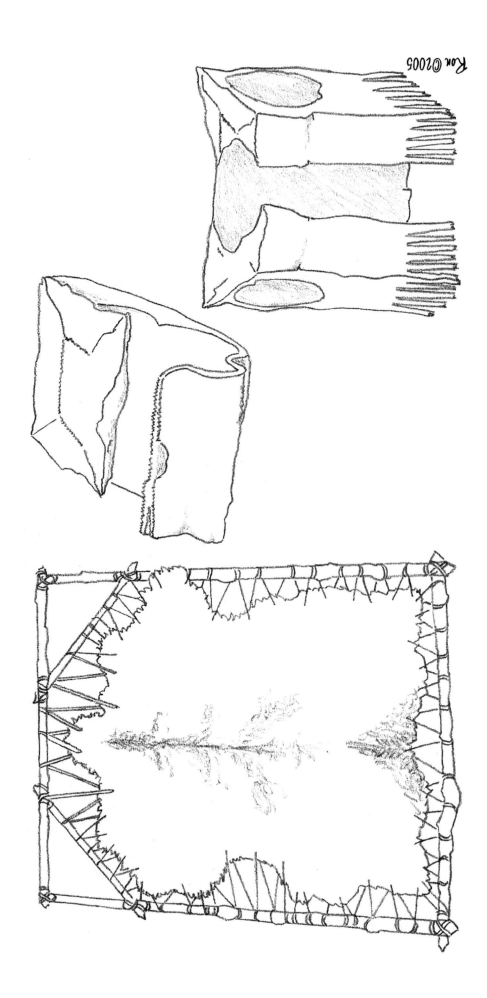

Ron @2005

Ron ©2005

Name

Name

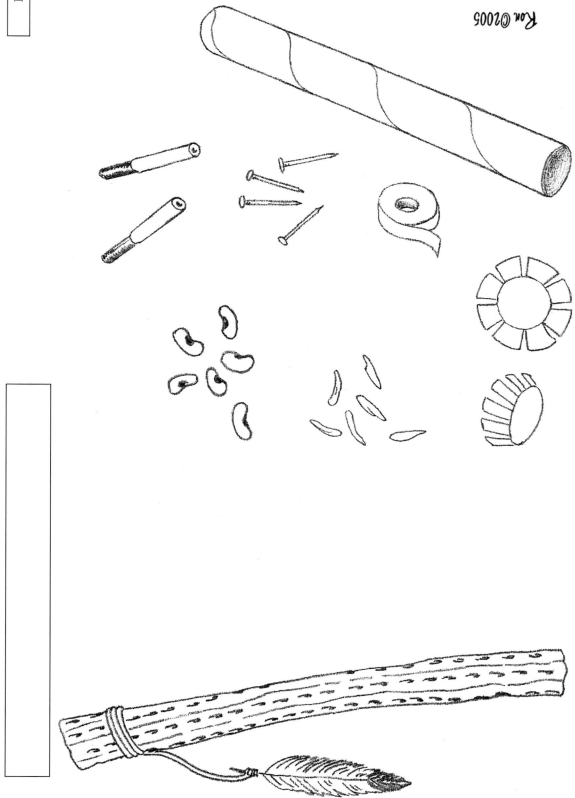

Ron @2005

Name

Ballot

Vote Today

VOTE Ballot Here

Name

Name

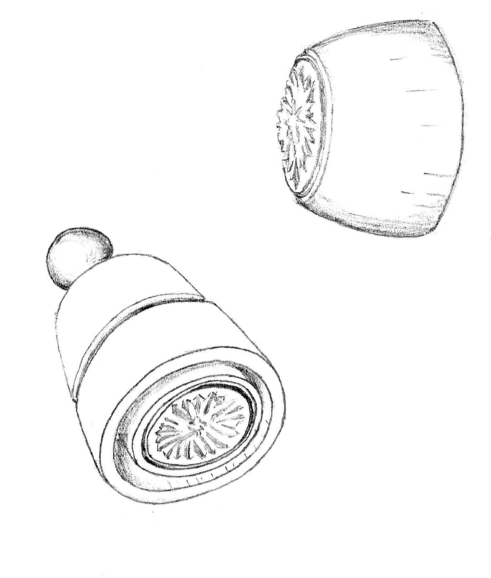

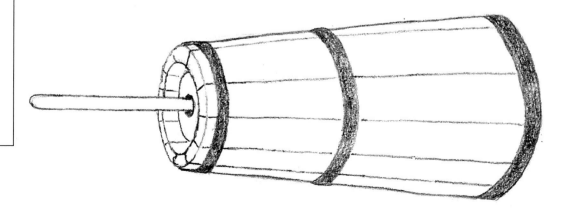

Name

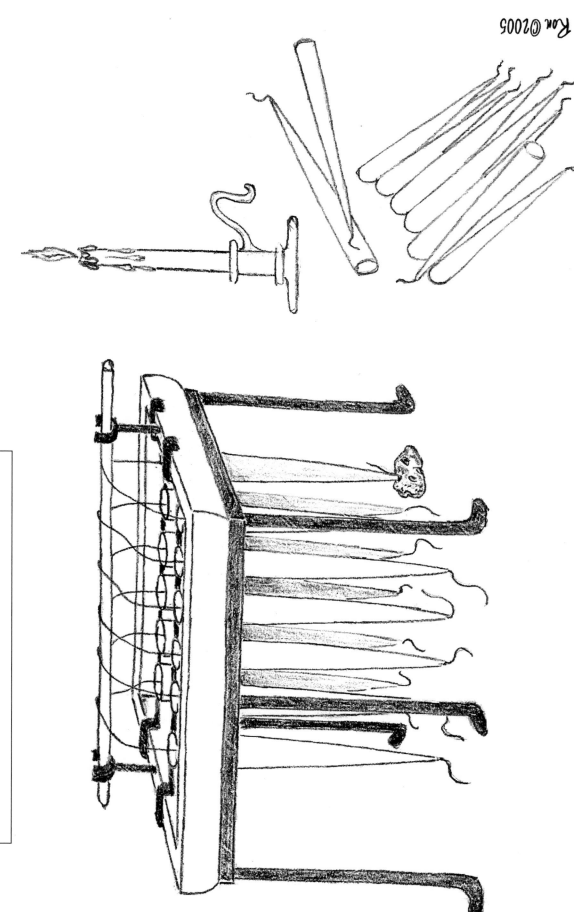

Name

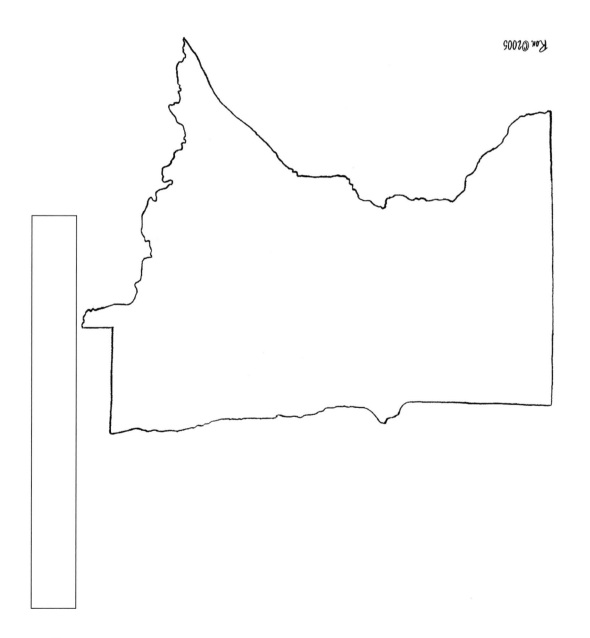

Minnesota

Ron @2005

Name

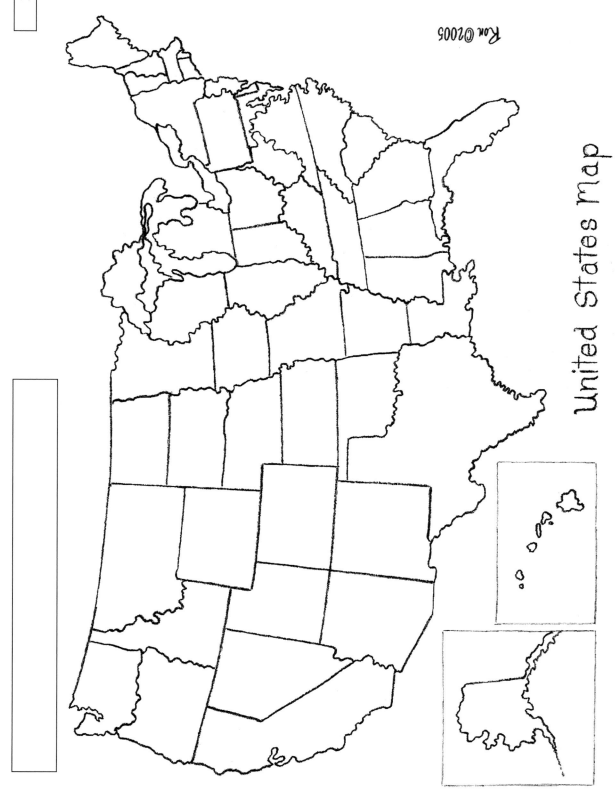

United States Map

Ron @2005

Name

Name

Ron @2005

Name

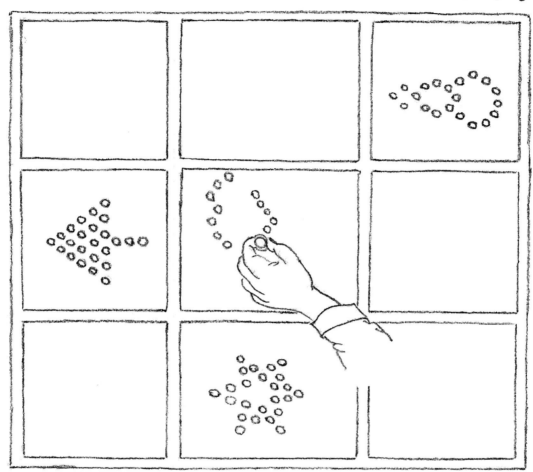

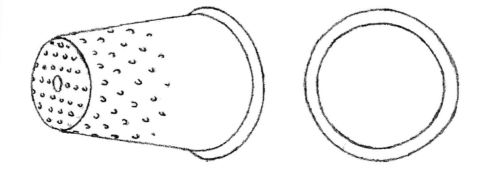

Name

Ron @2005

Name

Ron @2005

Name

Ron @2005

Name

Ron @2005

Name

Ron ©2005

Name

Name

Ron @2005

Name

Name

Ron ©2005

Name

Syllables

Ron @2005

Name

Ron ©2005

Name

Spelling Bee

apple
belt
cucumber
ditch
egg
finish
glasses
hair

indian
jelly
kitten
lamp
mouse
nest
open
pumpkin

quail
rabbit
sky
turtle
under
violin
well
yellow

Name

Ron ©2005

Name

Name

Ron @2005

Name

Ron ©2005

Name

Ron @2005

Name

Ron ©2005

Name

Ron @2005

Name

ISBN 1-41206013-3

9 781412 060134